WAKE UP RUNNING

DAVID EGEE

Copyright © 2014, David Egee. All rights reserved.
This publication may not be reproduced, stored in a retrieval system, or transmitted in whole or in part, in any form or by any means, electronic, mechanical, photocopying, recording, or otherwise, without the written permission of Editions Tilleul. Brief quotations may be used in professional articles or reviews, relevant research papers, or studies.

An Editions Tilleul Publication

The publisher made all reasonable efforts to contact all literature sources quoted in the text.

Editions Tilleul
PO Box 302
Bayside, CA 95524
www.editionstilleul.com

ISBN: 978-0-9896540-3-6

Book cover design by Gerd Borchgrevink, Logotyper as, Oslo, Norway

WAKE UP RUNNING

"When the lion wakes up in the morning, he has to run to catch the gazelle. When the gazelle gets up in the morning, he has to run to save his life. When the gazelle or the lion gets up in the morning, he must wake up running."

~ Old Arab Proverb

To Our Children
Cece, Tony, Adam, and Eliza

This book features many different people and places that shaped my life. After finishing the book, I realized that my professional commitments kept me out of my children's lives for long periods of time. As a result, I was unable to provide the necessary stability and support that might have helped them optimize their talents. While my wife and I concentrated on achieving our own goals, their lives were a case of simple survival.

~ David Egee, London 2014

ACKNOWLEDGEMENTS

Paul Wheeler
Annette Rabaiotti
Aziza Fahim
Divna Zarko Gaković
and
Peter Huhne

Contents

Prologue	1
Family, Friends, and Newtown	5
K Through 12	33
College	63
First Steps	77
The Middle East	103
England	163
Towards the End	177
Epilogue	195

Prologue

My father was about to get in the car to make his regular afternoon house calls when my mother called out, "Mrs. Lockwood is on the phone. Her son has just shot somebody and she thinks he's dead. What should she do?"

"Nothing," my father said, jumping into the car. I got in with him. As we drove to the Lockwood house, his face betrayed not a flicker of emotion. It wasn't the first gunshot wound he had attended. In those days in rural Connecticut, it was not unusual to have a rifle.

When we arrived, the boy was lying in the backseat of Mrs. Lockwood's car, blood all over him and the seat. He and his brother, Ronald, had been playing in a barn, where they found an ancient flintlock musket behind some old farm equipment. Ronald picked up the gun, jokingly pointed it at his friend and pulled the trigger. It was loaded.

When my father saw the boy, he asked Mrs. Lockwood to get some cotton. She brought a white sheet, which he then ripped into strips as if it were paper, strapped him up, and told her to take him to the emergency room. "I'll call ahead; they'll be expecting you," he said.

Walking back to the car, my father put his arm on my shoulder and said, "That boy will be dead by the time he gets to the hospital."

As long as I can remember, I always wanted to go wherever my father went. "David," he said, "I need to attend a postmortem on a guy at the hospital — want to come with me?" Although I was only seven years old at the time, I followed him whenever I could. His standard explanation for my presence was: "This is my son, David. Do you mind if he sits with me?" He would then suggest that I sit over to the side. I knew if I wanted to be with him, I had to behave — to be invisible. I can't remember anyone objecting, but in those days the doctor was God and the nuns were angels. Was I just lucky? Or did I take advantage of situations that were available to me? I had only to accept his invitation.

I grew up in the small, idyllic, rural community of Newtown, Connecticut. My education began in the four-room Sandy Hook School — made world famous 63 years later by the wanton murder of 20 students, four adults, and the suicide of the shooter.

I could hardly read or write, but I got through five schools, two colleges, and four universities. My career started in the state of Washington, the first in a long list of new locations and jobs: New Jersey, Alaska, Beirut, Rome, Dubai, Libya, and finally England — where I became a British subject. Several highlights in my career:

- Director of a 400-bed American University of Beirut Teaching Hospital, a rare opportunity. Before the civil war, Beirut was commonly referred to as the Switzerland of the Middle East. I worked with the most highly-trained doctors in the Middle East at that time, dealing with diplomats, spies, assassins, commandos, terrorists (depending on your political views);
- Advisor to the Ministry of Health in Saudi Arabia and Libya; and
- Collaborator with Dr. Donald Taeke Bosch, one of the last remaining missionary doctors in the Middle East, the physician who delivered the current Sultan of Oman,

Qaboos bin Said. I accompanied him on a very special trip to Muscat, Oman.

After escaping the civil war in Beirut by hitchhiking a ride on the Alitalia flight with the staff of the Italian Embassy, our family arrived in Rome, completely lost. A tightly knit unit while we lived in Beirut, the family was forced to scatter to five different countries.

Living in Rome was interesting; Dubai was a holiday. Libya was hell. Then, we moved to England and it became our home. We arrived in 1979, five months after Margaret Thatcher's election as Prime Minister. Heading the new conservative government, she encouraged the inclusion of private medicine in certain areas of the famous National Health Service (NHS). Working with Hospital Corporation of America (HCA), I was instrumental in establishing nine small provincial hospitals and four nursing homes in the UK. After ten years with HCA, I "cashed in my chips" and started DaleCare, my own nursing home company. Later, through a merger with another nursing home company, we created 50 homes situated throughout England and Scotland. After 12 years, I again "cashed in my chips" and retired at the age of 69.

Five years ago our daughter Eliza said "Papi, you should write a book."

Family, Friends, and Newtown

On Christmas day 1936 at home in Newtown, Connecticut, my mother went into labor. My father, a doctor, had gone to the hospital in Danbury to deliver a patient's baby (the customer always comes first). My mother had to call a neighbor, Smitty, who managed the local movie theatre. He took my mother to Bridgeport Hospital while his wife looked after my sister Elaine, who was born around the time my father graduated from medical school in 1934. I was delivered at 5:00 AM on the day after Christmas.

David

After spending seven days in the hospital, the usual length of stay in those days, I returned to Newtown, where I lived until I was sent to boarding school 12 years later. My earliest memories are of the rented house in which my father set up his General Medical Practice. The house had recently been built by the owner, a carpenter named Ronny Olson, and was located on a hill along the main road leading into the town center. My father was so impressed by the quality of the workmanship that three years later, he would ask Mr. Olson to build the house my parents lived in for the next 40 years.

We moved to our new home on the day the Japanese bombed Pearl Harbor, December 7, 1941. Sixty-five years later our house would be torn down to make way for a new commercial center, which included — ironically enough — a large Japanese restaurant.

My brother John and I shared an "indestructible" boy's room. The only pieces of movable furniture were two chairs. Bunk beds lined two opposite walls and a long worktable, with plenty of shelf space, was built into the third wall. A large set of heavy pinewood drawers, starting at floor level, ran along the other wall. I am sure my father designed it in the manner that he would have liked as a young boy, nearly maintenance free — which my mother liked. I had model airplanes hanging from the ceiling and pictures of military aircraft on all four walls. I loved airplanes and, 49 years later, I would get my pilot's license.

My brother and I could choose whichever bed we wanted. I chose the bed just below a window that looked out onto a large tree growing alongside the house. I remember exactly why I selected that bed: if ever there was a fire, I would be able to jump out of the window, climb down the tree, and save myself. My father told me in later years that I was always a worrier and to this day I continue to be. Although I was mindful (but not necessarily fearful) of what might happen, it never stopped me from doing the things I always wanted to do, even though I was always aware that something could go wrong. I grew up worrying about my grades in school, my parents getting a divorce, getting a young lady pregnant, failing exams, losing a job, and not having enough money to live the way I wanted.

As a worrier, I thought I wouldn't have anything more to worry about when I retired. But that isn't so. Now I worry about dying and death. Half-jokingly, I'd tell my colleagues at work that it was "guilt, worry, and stress" that got me up every morning, and it was also the cause of any successes I had in life.

The house with its large lawn was set on an acre of land. There was a large cornfield at the back, a hayfield and vegetable garden on one side, and a neighbor's house with an orchard on the other. Running along the front was the main road, Route 6, leading from Danbury to New Haven. The entire perimeter was my first playground. Wherever I went I pulled an old wagon behind me. It was bent in the middle and nearly touched the ground.

At a right angle to the main road was Uncle Herbert's farm. He had five cows, a horse, four or five pigs, and a couple of barn cats. Across the street was the town's public school. When I was six, I could cross the road by myself to start my first year of schooling.

One day, when I was between the age of five and six, while pulling my bent wagon, I complained that my right arm hurt. I also had a very high fever. My father took me to a pediatric colleague at Danbury Hospital, but no diagnosis could be made. The pain was not sharp; it was a dull throbbing. I sat on my bed at night, rocking and rocking against the wall, the way a lunatic in an insane asylum rocks in order to pass the time. The pain was excruciating. In the beginning, aspirin seemed to help, but finally when I could bear the pain no longer I went to my parents' bedroom to wake my father. I knew that he was a good doctor, but not a particularly compassionate one. Just as he had not been spoiled, he didn't spoil his children. When we were very young, we never went into our parents' bedroom at night — not because of bad dreams or to be cuddled or comforted. Going into their bedroom in the middle of the night was like, I imagine, going into a sleeping bear's cave. They slept in a high four-poster bed (later willed to our daughter Eliza).

"Dad? Dad," I whispered softly.

No response.

Finally my mother awoke and punched my father on the shoulder. "Benton, for gosh sakes, wake up. David is really suffering."

In a slightly grumpy way, he took me to the medicine cabinet in his office. He gave me two pills — not the customary pink aspirin — and said, "Try these." We went back to bed. He didn't say, "Take these and go back to sleep," so I thought he left it open for me to go back a second time. I did and then he gave me an injection, which I assumed was some kind of "special medicine." The next day we went to the Bridgeport Hospital to see a surgeon, Dr. Griswold, who made the preliminary diagnosis of osteomyelitis, an infection of the bone that occurs for no apparent reason. However, my mother, as was her nature, knew exactly what had caused it. "Benton, it's from him pulling that darn bent wagon everywhere he goes."

Osteomyelitis is an infection that enters the bloodstream and settles in a particular area of the bone, usually the tibia, femur, ankle, or arm. In my case it affected my right arm. The body's defense system causes pus to form, which eats into the bone, creating an abscess that then spreads throughout the bone. When the infection goes into the bone, there's no room for the swelling it causes. As the infection increases, it puts tremendous pressure on the bone. Only with surgery can the infection be drained, which happens over a period of days. The incision is deliberately held open to allow the drainage to take place and leaves a very broad scar when it finally heals. Today both my arms have large, obvious scars.

I have a very vivid memory of lying on a stretcher and being pushed by someone I could see only from under his chin. It seemed like rather a long ride. From the darkened corridor, we entered a brightly-lit, tiled operating theatre. Two huge lamps resembling searchlights hung from the ceiling with additional light streaming in from large glass windows running high along one of the walls. People talked among themselves in very serious, low tones. Suddenly, a cloth was pushed to my nose with one hand while another kept my mouth closed. There was a terrible, sickening smell of ether. I tried to kick, but I couldn't. I tried to push, but I couldn't move. There must have been four people holding me down. The only thing I could do was turn my head slightly from one side to the other, but the ether-soaked rag kept following me.

When I was diagnosed with the disease in 1940, the survival rate among young children was only 10 percent. At the time, the only treatment for osteomyelitis was sulphonamide drugs, which were the forerunners of the first anti-microbiological drugs that would eventually pave the way for the antibiotic revolution. The doctors started treating me with sulphonamide drugs, but they became a very real problem. The drug, when taken in large doses as was required in my case, caused urinary tract and hemophilia disorders. Therefore, if the osteomyelitis didn't kill me, the drugs certainly could because large doses in children were always lethal. The only thing I can remember is being forced to drink large quantities of water in an effort to stop kidney failure. I also remember being awakened throughout the night by one of the nurses in order to drink water in addition to being given intravenous liquids.

Dr. Griswold felt that my best and only chance of survival was to try to obtain a new commercially-produced drug called penicillin. This was during World War II, so, at the time, all manufactured penicillin was sent directly to the War Department to treat wounded military personnel, as well as the GIs returning from overseas who were being looked after in the various veterans' hospitals throughout the country. One of Dr. Griswold's patients was the mayor of Bridgeport (the only mayor to successfully run on a Socialist party ticket). Dr. Griswold used his influence with the mayor to obtain the penicillin from the veterans' hospital in Bridgeport. According to the literature I've read, "The effect that penicillin may have on an individual can be detected within six to eight hours of being administered." My father went to the veterans' hospital, got the medicine, returned to Dr. Griswold's, and then returned home to find that my mother's friend Corinne was visiting. He said to them, "If he lives through the night, in all likelihood he will survive."

When Corinne left to go home, she passed Saint Rose's Catholic Church on the way. Being a good Catholic and a strong believer, she stopped to light a candle and pray for my life. Corinne had a daughter, Dale, whom I married 22 years later. She gives her mother full credit for my survival.

I can't say that the disease stopped me from doing anything I wanted to do. Although I was thin and not as strong as I should have been, I was well coordinated, agile, competitive, and enthusiastic about most things in life. I usually made the team in various sports. What I lacked in natural athletic abilities I made up for in effort and enthusiasm. I never used my osteomyelitis as an excuse for not doing something; even while recovering in the hospital, I was able to manage a wheelchair with only one arm.

My hero at the time was a baseball player named Mickey Mantle, who played center field for the New York Yankees for 18 years. He was able to play all during the war because he was exempt from the draft, having contracted osteomyelitis in high school. He survived the disease but died at the age of 68, an alcoholic with a diseased liver.

Osteomyelitis consumes most of my early memories. I had continued bouts but as penicillin became more widely available, the treatment of future episodes became more predictable. In the early days of penicillin, it was given by mouth. I would take it in a small shot-glass measure, four times a day. It was yellow in color and absolutely foul in both smell and taste. A short shiver ran through my body after taking it, but I would immediately be given an Oreo cookie to get rid of the dreadful taste that I imagined was close to the taste of ammonia or urine. Of course, I've never actually tasted urine, but I use it to describe the taste of penicillin to others.

A few years ago, our daughter's partner, a doctor at the Columbia Presbyterian Hospital in New York City, explained to me that I was, in fact, drinking urine. In the early days, penicillin patients required huge dosages because the drug would pass through the body within three or four hours. Because of the primitive methods available to manufacturers, only small amounts were available at any given time. Hence, urine was collected from the penicillin patients. The antibiotic was then filtered from the urine but small amounts still remained, which explained the look and the taste. I had my last operation at the age of 32, when I was the director of the American University

Hospital in Beirut, but I owed my timely recovery to drinking the urine of the soldiers at Bridgeport veterans' hospital.

Father

My father always referred to himself as J. Benton Egee.

The sign placed next to the highway in front of our house, read: "J. Benton Egee, MD." Dad was never "John" and rarely "Ben." My mother always referred to him as Benton — never "dear" or "darling."

From the few details I've uncovered, I have to conclude that his early childhood was not a happy part of his life. He was born in 1907 and raised in Frankfurt, Philadelphia, where he attended medical school. He lived for 90 years. He had a sister and one brother who were 10 years and 11 years younger than he was. I only met them once in my life — at my mother's funeral.

Dad's father never had a steady job. He never made it clear to me exactly what his father did, if anything. He only told me once: "We used to move from house to house a lot." When they did move, it was always for a "better opportunity," but it never seemed so to my father. "He was always getting a new job, but never a better job," he once told me. Even while my father was working his way through college and medical school, his father asked to borrow money in order to pay his rent, which always upset my father. But if he didn't help, it meant his mother would have to move again. While writing this book, I discovered three letters he wrote to her that gave me the impression he was very close to her. The only thing he told me about his mother was that she was not very strong and that she died from cancer soon after he graduated from medical school in 1934 at the age of 29, which was around the time my parents moved from Philadelphia to Newtown, Connecticut.

I remember a conversation between my parents regarding Dad's father. "Well, he's passing right by the house. You've got to at least invite him in," Mom said. It was a very short visit during which my grandfather complained that he had to walk up a flight of stairs to use the toilet.

On another occasion, I recall my mother asking my father what she should send his father for Christmas. I distinctly remember his reply:
"Nothing."
"Oh, Benton, you've got to send something," she said.
"Send him a box of cigars."
"But that's what you sent last year."
"Well, he was lucky."
"What's his address?"
"I have no idea."

I knew a lot about my mother's parents. They came to stay with us every Christmas, and on a number of occasions, my sister and I stayed with them in a row house on Leaper Street in Frankfurt, Philadelphia. Living nearby were two second cousins, with whom I still remain in contact (one has since died). When my grandfather retired as a machinist, my father built my mother's parents a house in the large field next to our house in Newtown. Their names were Ernest and Agnes. But they were always referred to as Jake and Ag. Since my own retirement, I miss my grandfather more than ever. Since he was a skilled, untrained craftsman — I would love to show him my workshop and ask for his help.

While in medical school, my father had a summer job as a milkman with a horse and wagon. One of his customers was a very kind, friendly woman. She was old for her age, bent over at nearly a 45-degree angle with rheumatoid arthritis of the spine. She showed kindness and warmth equally — be it towards a milkman or a bank manager. In spite of being bent over, she was ready to help anyone, at any time. Although uneducated, she was intelligent and curious. Her husband, Jake, a machinist, provided for their family with a modest income. She always said good morning to my father when he delivered the milk and gradually convinced him to stay for a cup of coffee and a biscuit. One day, her daughter was at the house. After a few more routine milk deliveries, he summoned the nerve to ask her out on a date.

Mother

As long as I can remember, my mother, Gladys (an old-fashioned name, which I never liked), was always described by her family and friends as being "quite beautiful" — and I think she knew this. She went to the hairdresser's all the time. When she visited us in Beirut, she told my wife that she had never shampooed her own hair. She never walked in anything except high heels, and that included her bedroom slippers. Whether going to the grocery store, or going to Amaral's Garage to fill the car with gas, she left the house only after her mid-day shower. She was endowed with an exceptional sense of taste that was reflected not only in her dress style but in the decoration of our home, as well.

Among her friends and guests, she was known as being an excellent hostess and cook. During dinner parties, Elaine and I used to sit on the steps listening to their laughter and bits of conversation. I liked whenever they had guests because sitting on the steps after bedtime made us feel included.

My mother came from a modest background. Her father was a builder, who became a machinist in a very large munitions factory that she always referred to as "the arsenal." He was never without work. It helped, I suppose, having World War II, then the Korean and Vietnam Wars.

I don't think my mother graduated from high school. Although she never mentioned it, she was, in today's parlance, dyslexic. Schooling was exceedingly difficult for her and she never finished. All I ever learned about that period of her life was that she had an aunt who sold tickets at the local Philadelphia movie theatre, so she spent her afternoons and evenings at the movies.

Even though my mother never completed her education, I think she survived successfully by natural instinct — street smarts. At an early age, she imagined what her future would be and filled the role splendidly, as if she had followed a script. When a milkman working his way through medical school asked this then 16-year-old girl out on a date one summer, she was ready to play the part she had imagined for herself. The following year my parents were married, remaining so until my mother's death at age 80.

In Newtown, Mom was very popular among her many friends, who were, for the most part, other housewives. Some were also professional women; others were married to famous people such as Elia Kazan. All, except my mother, were college educated. Quite unusual for the times, she not only fit in, she excelled.

My father loved intellectual discussions involving political issues, cultural events, or psychological concepts. He thought and talked on an abstract level. He was very intelligent, very knowledgeable, and always interested in new ideas or new ways to solve problems. My poor mother could not satisfy this need nor could she respond accordingly. Now and then an argument would break out. It never occurred to my father that she was not on his intellectual level. As soon as the discussion started, my sister and I knew how it would end. One time, he became so impatient and irate that he took a bottle of wine and banged it on the table, hoping that breaking the neck would silence her, but the bottle wouldn't break.

When I was 17, late one night and quite by accident, I caught them in a compromising situation that led me to believe that their quarrels were usually settled in bed. As a young child, after their clashes I thought to myself: *If they divorce, I definitely want to live with my father.* He was such a positive influence in my life; I was much closer to him than my mother.

For 20 years my mother managed and succeeded in her life as the wife of a successful country doctor. For those 20 years, she did as Jackie Stewart — the famous and severely dyslexic race car driver — who wrote, "I managed to get around things I needed to do."

While my mother managed very well, her secret was ultimately discovered while acting as a navigator for my father on a motor tour around England. He discovered that she was unable to read the road signs. He was quite surprised. I'll never forget the time he told me, "You know, I don't think your mother can read."

Had I realized the extent of her handicap, I would have been more sympathetic. How hard she must have worked to deal with everyday life! And having a well-educated husband and friends, who were more culturally inclined, only made the situation more problematic. To survive, she had to wake up running.

Paul

The youngest of five siblings, Paul was born ten years after I was. I believe he had a difficult time growing up because he was out of sync with the rest of the children. I always thought of Paul as an inconvenience. Soon after he was brought home from the hospital, I had my first serious talk with my father. I had just taken the garbage out, and my sister was hanging up the newly washed diapers. I asked my father if I could move into Uncle Herbert's barn just across the road. He took this request quite seriously, asking calmly why I wanted to do that. I explained that I did not want another little brother and would prefer to live somewhere else. He asked how I was planning to feed myself.

"I will live in the barn and have my meals with Uncle Herbert and Aunt Sarah," I said.

"What will you do about Christmas? Where are you going to spend Christmas Eve? Won't you feel lonely and left out of your family?" He suggested I talk with Uncle Herbert and think about it a little more. Obviously, I never mentioned it again.

I always felt Paul was distant from the rest of us. I had established a very close relationship with my sister, Elaine, who was 18 months older than me. My younger brother and sister were also close, so Paul was left out. When I did include him, it was because my mother nagged me to the point where it was easier to just go along. Perhaps I felt a little sorry for him.

He was not athletic at all, he didn't roughhouse, and he wasn't rambunctious like other boys his age. Instead, he was fearful and avoided team sports completely. I suppose to any other ten-year-old boy, he was a sissy, but we never called him that — I guess because he was our brother. I just thought he was different. He went away to boarding school when he was 13 or 14, but only stayed a year.

I think Paul and I had our first intelligent conversation when he was home for holiday from an art college that he was attending in Arkansas. He amused me with his entertaining stories and was very knowledgeable about art. He had good taste and style. My appreciation for Paul grew when Dale and I married; they both had a mutual interest in the arts, which I think helped me to establish a new relationship with him. The arts brought them together and hence me. Paul became an excellent interior designer (Paul Newman and Joanne Woodward were among his clients). Today, I regret my indifference and hope we'll talk about it one day.

John

My second brother was two years younger than I. He was named after my father, but was always called John or Johnny. I never got along with him either, but throughout our lives, we have maintained an "armed truce," a guarded respect for one another since we shared the same bedroom until I went to boarding school. We had nothing in common. I don't remember ever having a fight with him, either physically or verbally. Rather, we lived together like a cat and dog that live in harmony, but at a distance. He was not at all athletic and was socially shy within the family environment. He, too, went to boarding school for one year, didn't particularly like it, and graduated from the local high school. John spent four years in the US Air Force. He left the service with the same rank he had when he entered. I didn't think that was possible.

During those four years, he spent most of his time in Korea, staring at a radar screen and drinking cheaply-priced whisky from the subsidized PX. He once said to me that he drank his lifetime allowance of whisky during his years in the Air Force.

John spent two years studying hotel management, but instead became a mink ranch farmer and then a heavy equipment landscape operator. He was, as I imagined, a certain type of frontier man. He lived in the woods, built his own house, fixed his own car, and helped his neighbors when they were in trouble. As I grew older, I began to appreciate him for who he was. When he retired at the age of 63, he got a grant from the State of Massachusetts to attend a truck driving school in order to get a license to drive juggernauts (16-wheelers). I envied him because I always had notions of being a truck driver. I remember telling my wife that if there is a life after death, I wanted to be a women's fashion designer, an airplane pilot, or a truck driver.

We had made plans for me to take a two-week holiday and accompany him across America in an articulated truck. Sadly, only a few weeks after obtaining his license, my brother was diagnosed with lung cancer and died soon afterwards.

John was a very popular member of his community — if anyone needed help, advice about the local area, or was in need of "insider information," they could go to "Brother John." He even ploughed the local roads for his neighbors during the winter because they were not part of the state's highway system. When he died, his local town commissioned the State of Massachusetts to name a road after him. Egee Drive was registered and thereafter the State plowed his namesake road in the winter, enabling John to rest in peace.

Leslie

My second sister, Leslie, was six years younger than I. As with my other siblings, I had very little in common with her, partly because I started going to boarding schools when she was about six. We spent very little time together so we never really knew each other very well. She recently said, "My best memory of David is that he was never there."

When Leslie was very young, I think she wanted to be a boy. She must have observed that her three male siblings had an easier life than she did. Boys were never expected to wash dishes, make beds, do laundry, sweep or hang out wash (except in the winter). Obviously, she envied our position in the family. As she grew older, and when my sister Elaine went off to boarding school, helping my mother with domestic chores fell completely on her shoulders. My mother depended more and more on her. Sometimes, she was forced to interrupt her social life in order to assist in the household. Looking back, I felt she was treated like Cinderella — left behind while her two stepsisters went to the ball. I felt sorry for her, but never did anything to rectify the situation.

Leslie was "outdoorsy" and enthusiastic. She liked to join my father in outdoor activities such as skeet and trap shooting, and hunting. While in nurses' training she had to learn the technique for restarting a heart, which involved suddenly pounding on the patient's chest. In real life, she was faced with just such a situation. She successfully used the technique, but in her enthusiasm, broke two of the patient's ribs.

She married a wonderful man of few words, who listened very carefully, a nice balance to her exuberance and outgoing personality. He was a professional farmer in Minnesota, rearing pigs with zero acres under cultivation. In a friendly rural farming community, Leslie found her place in life and excelled. She raised two boys, who left the farm to become successful in their chosen professions. At the same time, she was able to continue her nursing career, finally ending it as an instructor.

In some ways I envy her; she found a place to call home in a community of people she enjoyed, a far cry from the East Coast mores of Connecticut.

Elaine

Older than me by 18 months, Elaine was my best friend in the whole family and the longest-standing best friend of my entire life. When we were very small, whenever she had bad dreams she used to climb into my bed in the middle of the night. Later, Elaine and her friend, Judy Gutman, initiated me in the game of "You show me yours; I'll show you mine." As unforgettable as that experience is for young children, it was never discussed. When Elaine and I went to the movies at the local town hall or walked to the village coffee shop or the chemist, I used to imagine she was my girlfriend. She grew up quickly — she was aware of her sexuality at a very early age and had a close relationship with a married man nearly twice her age when she was only 15. He managed the town hall movie theatre for the night performances and she babysat his infant child. I don't know if their relationship was ever consummated. My father found out about it and discussed it with Elaine — not in a scolding way, but in a concerned, parental manner. It was then that my father decided to send her off to boarding school. Oddly enough, he sent her to a Quaker co-educational school in New York. When she came home for a Thanksgiving holiday, she brought her then boyfriend. My father liked playing golf and thought he was a pretty good weekend player. Her boyfriend, however, proceeded to beat him rather badly. I'm not sure whether it was the golf or the guy, but he moved Elaine to the Walnut Hill School, an all-girls school in Framingham, Massachusetts.

I liked all of her boyfriends and envied the seemingly confident way that she managed her relationships with the opposite sex. As they grew older and had cars (in Connecticut you could drive at 16), she used to invite me to come along on some of her dates when they went to the movies in nearby Danbury. Afterwards, we would have a hamburger and vanilla milkshake together at Dirkuns Diner on White Street. We would then go home and I'd go directly to bed. After a movie date, she and her boyfriend would sit on the sofa in the living room while our parents slept upstairs.

I was pleased that she included me as much as she could. From them, I learned the dating rules according to the prep school code — how to behave and act with a girlfriend, what to talk about, and how to dress. What I didn't learn from her boyfriends, I learned from Playboy — at that time, a new magazine. I thought her lifestyle was exactly what I wanted mine to be.

At the age of 20, and after two years at Wells College, she married her husband, Peter, a quiet, self-assured, and introspective fellow; and a Harvard graduate. Like my father, Peter enjoyed hunting and fishing. They went on a number of trips together, and hence, got along very well. My father enjoyed Peter's company and appreciated the advantages that his family was able to provide him. However, he was concerned that Peter did not have a specific goal in mind at this time in his life. In their conversations together, and with an eye on his own daughter's future, my father encouraged him to try medical school. Peter became head of one of the medical departments at Mount Sinai Hospital in New York. He later joined my father in creating a new medical emergency room service in Danbury; and later Peter developed his own independent health center.

At the time of this writing, Elaine and Peter have been married for 40 years with a two-year separation during which my sister lived in a yurt brought over from Tibet. Elaine and Peter created a wonderful lifestyle that included a Purdy shotgun leaning in a corner of the living room; and, a coffee table stacked with copies of *Field and Stream*, the *National Review*, and *The New Yorker*. On a large black sofa was a mink-skin throw blanket with red trim. Everything was early Ralph Lauren, the kind of environment I thought I wanted. A little chaotic and very "lived-in," it was unlike our mother's house that was "magazine-cover perfect."

Uncle Herbert

Uncle Herbert lived almost directly across the road from our house. He was not a real uncle, but we always referred to him as though he was. He was my first connection with anyone outside my family, the reason I crossed the road for the first time. Uncle Herbert came from an old, New England family. He was a farmer and a part-time rural postman. He was single and lived in a typical New England family house with his father and unmarried sister. The house was constructed of clapboard and painted white with long, black shutters. It had a deep porch that ran along the front and side of the house, making it appear even bigger. It had a 19th century kitchen where Uncle Herbert's father sat by the wood-burning stove in a rocking chair when he wasn't doing farm chores. The family of three lived in that house their entire lives, until they all gradually died. It was then turned into lawyers' offices and remains so to this date.

When I was young, the farm consisted of only a few cows, a handful of pigs and Dolly, a huge old white draught horse. In some respects, the family continued to live a 19th-century life. They made their own soap and candles, and they canned fruits and vegetables from their garden.

Every year, they slaughtered one of the pigs. I witnessed the slaughter and carving up of a pig on one occasion. I remember it like it was yesterday. It was beginning to get dark when they started, so they lit the area with the tractor's headlamps, which made the event even more dramatic, like a scene from a horror movie. The slaughter took place in one corner of a muddy pigpen surrounded by a heavy wooden fence. The high-pitched screaming from the pig as they tried to slit its throat was unforgettable.

One of the men was an itinerant butcher who went from farm to farm cutting up pigs. When the pig was killed, Uncle Herbert and the other man strung it up on a special frame so that the butcher could carve up the entire animal after cutting out the offal. It was frightening but I could not stop watching; I was paralyzed. The three men shouted orders to one another and talked loudly throughout the procedure. They were either cursing the pig, demanding help, or needing something here or something there. It was probably the most violent event I had ever witnessed in my life. The blood, the entrails, the trauma, and the lighting all created an unforgettable scene. To this day, whenever I pass the large pig farms in Gloucestershire and Devonshire, I think back to that autumn night in Connecticut.

Uncle Herbert had a horse-drawn buggy and horse-drawn snow sled, which sat gathering dust in the far end of his barn. The harnesses were attached to the wall nearby. They had not been used for many years. On Christmas Eve, my parents traditionally had an open house party for friends and neighbors. They produced a large leg of ham, probably from Uncle Herbert, along with German potato salad made by my grandmother. At some point during the evening, the children would be sent up to bed. My father then phoned Uncle Herbert to tell him that we were in bed. Just before we went to sleep, Uncle Herbert would walk along the pavement leading to our front door shaking the sleigh bells of his horse's harness. He banged on the front door and when my father opened, he would say, "Ho! Ho! Ho! Merry Christmas!"

"Santa, you have to come back later because the children just went to bed," my father would reply.

"Ho! Ho! Ho! I'll be back."

And then we would hear sleigh bells as he walked away. I must have been the last person in my class who still believed in Santa Claus. I got into arguments about it with some of my classmates. Before I embarrassed myself any further, our teacher, Mrs. Gaffney, took me aside and explained that Santa Claus wasn't real.

When my siblings and I decided to have a group photo taken 20 years later, we agreed that the inside of Herbert's barn would be appropriate. After the photo session, we took a look around the barn. The horse-drawn buggy, the sleigh, and the harness with the sleigh bells were all still there.

When I was around 11, my father and Uncle Herbert decided to buy a horse from the local blacksmith who owned a quarter horse called Danny, which he used mostly for pulling wagons. My father was very keen on the idea, probably because it reminded him of when he worked his way through medical school selling milk off a horse-drawn wagon. He also thought it would be a good idea for the kids, me in particular, to use it for riding. Uncle Herbert wanted his old horse, Dolly, to have some company. So they bought Danny.

I was curious about the horse and at the time, I loved cowboys' and Indians' movies. I dreamed of being a cowboy when I grew up. To be frank, the idea of riding a horse myself was a little scary. But I couldn't tell my father I was afraid.

At first, I thought I could simply saddle up and ride like Roy Rogers or Gene Autry, whom I saw in the Saturday matinee B movies. In hindsight, the whole thing was a disaster. I was the one left to feed the horse and be "responsible." Trying to get a bridle on Danny was almost impossible. On the rare occasion that Uncle Herbert was present, he would easily saddle him up. I tried to imitate what he did, but he didn't take the time to teach me. In spite of my digging my heels into Danny, he walked along reluctantly, never doing what I wanted him to do.

I once mistakenly left the door of the feed storage area open while feeding Danny. To compound my error, I also left open the heavy lids of the metal containers in which the food was stored. Naturally, the cows and the horses got into the feed room. Horses, I later learned, eat until they're full. But cows eat until they get sick, and these certainly did. Dr. Russell Strasburger, the local vet and a close friend of my father's, was called. Uncle Herbert was furious. He grabbed me by the shirt collar, removed his hat, and started beating me over the head with it, all the time cursing me. I had never experienced such a punishment, except from my father. Even then, I was always warned that I was going to be spanked and forced to think about it. This particular beating was nothing like that.

My mother kept asking my father, "Benton, why don't you get rid of that darned horse?" That's the closest she ever got to swearing. Eventually, she had her way and Danny was passed on to a young girl in my class, Patricia Daniels. Her father was a gentleman farmer, and she was a typical farmer's daughter: pretty, but a tomboy. I remember how confident she seemed with the horse when we delivered it and how unafraid she was as she led him to his new barn. I liked her and would invite her out five years later for a date in my 1929 Ford Roadster. But it would be 33 years before I ever attempted to ride a horse again.

Al Boyson

In 1944, at the age of eight, I started working for Al Boyson of Boyson's Dairy, which was owned and operated by Al's mother and father. In 1956, when I graduated from Wooster School, I also graduated from Boyson's Dairy. It was the first summer in twelve years that I didn't work the milk route with Al. When I think back to the summers of my early childhood, the times I spent with him are the ones I remember best.

Every morning, I could see a milkman bring five quarts of milk to the side door of our house, just below my bedroom window. If I wasn't already awake, the clanging of the bottles would wake me. Al Boyson would occasionally have a young helper who was probably five years older than I was. I thought it would be fun to do that one day, and I imagined myself to be like the young helper.

In the summer months, I would get up early and sit on the top of an old gatepost in the empty pasture next to our home. When I saw Al's truck coming, I would jump down from the gatepost and run to it before he had a chance to step down. I'd bring the empty bottles to his truck and take the full ones back to our door. He used a wire basket with a wooden handle that carried up to six bottles. I managed four. I now sometimes see these baskets in antique shops, and they remind me of those summer mornings.

One day, Al agreed to let me "help him." After a short discussion between Al and my mother, it was agreed that I could go part of the way on his route. At each house, he would hand me the metal basket — never more than four bottles — and I would jump off the truck, deliver the bottles to the door and bring back the empties, placing them in the wooden cases at the back of the truck as he drove to the next house. This was repeated again and again throughout the day. I felt grown up. I was contributing, and I enjoyed the atmosphere. He taught me adult responsibility. I was doing what he would otherwise have to do. In those hours of the day, I felt grown up.

It wouldn't be long before he let me go on the entire route. He picked me up between seven and seven-thirty in the morning and dropped me back home about three in the afternoon. We used to have lunch at one of the four local diners or hamburger joints. I greatly disliked one snack bar in particular, a real greasy spoon near Lake Zoar that sold mostly hotdogs, hamburgers, french fries, and ice cream. The owner's stomach hung over the counter, and he was fat and sweaty in his dirty t-shirt.

"Why do we have to eat here, Al?" I asked.

He looked at me and said, "He's a customer. He buys our milk so we eat his hamburgers." Al paused, smiled, and added, "Sometimes."

That was my first lesson in customer relations.

As I got older, I left our house at about five-thirty in the morning during the summer and rode my bicycle the two miles to his farm. I helped his mother bottle the milk while he and his father milked their eight cows. Then Al and I would deliver the milk. At the end of the route, we would return to the farm, wash and sterilize the empty bottles, and tend to the farming chores. I learned how to use all of their farm equipment, which included a hay truck and two farm tractors with attached mowers and snow plows.

In the evenings, the cows would be milked again, mostly by machines, but a few by hand. The bottles would immediately be filled and placed in a huge refrigerator for delivery the next morning. I would return home anywhere between five and eight in the evening. My mother often complained, gently, about how terrible I smelled from all those "dirty cows."

"Get yourself upstairs to take your bath immediately," she would cry.

She would speak that way to my father, and she had the same manner whenever he came in from working in the garden or from a day of hunting. My father worked from nine to nine, so I would sometimes go days without seeing him. I felt grown up and liked it when my mother spoke to me that way. Being clean and tidy was part of the impression we were expected to give the outside world. But I always thought barns and cows smelled quite nice.

Al paid me each day at the end of the route with one dollar bills. My salary went from 15 cents to seven dollars a day over eight years. I didn't trust my brothers and sisters, and the bank was always closed whenever I needed to deposit my savings, so I needed places to hide my money. One place I hid it was in the ears of the stuffed deer's head, a trophy from one of my father's hunting trips. Deer ears hold a surprising amount of crumpled dollar bills.

Then there was an aluminum ice bucket on the highest shelf in the kitchen. I had to stand on the kitchen barstool and reach as far as I could just to grasp the bottom. I would crush the dollar bills into tight balls so the bucket looked full.

In those days, the mid-1940s, my father charged three dollars for an office visit and five dollars for house calls. Most of his patients paid in cash, invariably giving him a five or ten dollar bill. Often, my father would stick his head out of the office door into our kitchen and say to my mother, "Gladys, ask David for change of a tenner." When I gave my father ten tight balls of paper, he would have to undo each dollar bill. He went back into his office with a short explanation. I could only hear the first few words before the door slammed shut: "Sorry, but my son…"

I think he rather enjoyed telling people why the change was crumpled.

Al brought me into the grown-up world. He treated me like a small adult and I loved it. Over the next ten years, I would continue to work with him every school holiday, summer holiday, and some weekends throughout the year. Over the months and years, I became involved in Al's life to the point where I was spending more waking hours with him and his mother and father, helping with the chores, than I did with my own.

Al guided me through that critical period between 8 and 18. He told me what the distributor does in a car engine, proved that a Chevrolet was better than a Ford (except the Model A), and taught me how to fix a bicycle sprocket. Those were but a few of the crucial lessons learned.

Al also taught me all I needed to know about girls. He taught me to never try to kiss a girl on the first date if you really liked her; he told me about girls menstruating once a month, and he bought me my first Esquire magazine — the soft porn Playboy predecessor. I could talk to him about my early girlfriends. At what point should I kiss her? When was it all right to "feel her up"?

My formative years with Al were all about cars, work, and the dynamics of human relations, particularly with Kenny Shaw, the garbage man; the garage manager, Harry Greenman; the town sheriff, Hiney Hanlan; the manager of the feed store, Tony; and Joan, the pretty girl at the village coffee shop.

During the periods when work on the farm was not as intense, Al drove a bus for the Flying Eagle Bus Company, a small business headquartered in Danbury, Connecticut, about ten miles from Newtown. The bus routes included New York City, White Plains, and Hartford, with chartered trips to the surrounding area, including Yankee Stadium and the Polo Grounds.

The route to New York City was not very popular; the bus was rarely more than half full. Al would often invite me to come along for the ride to New York to keep him company. I would stand beside him to open and close the passenger door. The passengers were regular customers and he seemed to know most of them so there was always an opportunity for friendly small talk.

In New York City, there was a central bus depot for out-of-town buses. We drove into an underground tunnel. At the end was a big turntable that aligned the buses so they could dock in their assigned slots. About an hour later, we would start the return trip.

When we got back to the bus depot in Danbury, around ten-thirty at night, it was Al's routine to offer any attractive young lady a ride to her home. Sometimes he got lucky and was offered a cup of coffee. Sometimes he got even luckier.

There was a strict understanding that I would remain in the car. I had a vague understanding of why I wasn't included and I would usually just fall asleep. By the time I got home, my family would be asleep and I'd be back on the farm before they got up the next morning.

In hindsight, it seems quite incredible that my parents allowed me to take these trips. But my father was the Boyson family's doctor and knew Al's parents well. He knew, too, that Al was not irresponsible and that I was in safe hands.

I was taken in by Al's family and treated as a small person rather than a child. I was given real responsibilities. I came to understand my role in their family and what was expected of me. Life at the farm seemed to suit me very well: I learned new skills and I had a pretty good mechanical aptitude. Where school gave me anxiety, worry, and apprehension, being with Al gave me confidence. It was a relief from the torture of school, but I understood that the farm was only a reprieve — it was pretend life in contrast to school's real life.

Granted, farm work never challenged my intellect. I didn't like sitting in a tree and reading a book like Dale used to do. All I ever read were the captions under the pictures in the car magazines Al bought me, along with magazines about motorcycles and airplanes.

Al never read. His mother kept the books and seemed to be the brains of the family. His father couldn't read. The amount of reading and writing required on the farm was minimal. It was a doer's world rather than an academic's world. Doing chores on the farm was not looked upon as chores — it was just part of life. At home, chores almost seemed to be a punishment. "Don't just hang about, clean the garage," my mother would say.

A day on the farm wasn't nine to five. Farmers lived in their work environment; it was all around them. You didn't lock up the office and drive away, just as my father did not lock up his GP's office and drive away. The two men I most admired for totally opposite reasons — Al and my father — both woke up running, and they kept running the entire day.

When Al wasn't working at the farm, delivering milk, driving a bus, plowing a driveway in the winter, or mowing an empty field for some client in the summer, it was time for fun. On Saturday nights, we'd go to Bridgeport for the stock car races or to Danbury for the midget car races or to Hartford for the annual car show. But the most fun was simply to take a ride in Al's car — a 1950 Jaguar XK 120, the most desirable sports car in America at the time, of which there were very few. To drive with Al in that car was a thrilling experience for a 15-year-old. Open to the elements, the throaty hum of the motor, the car so tightly-sprung that you got the real feel of the road low to the ground — in fact, you could almost touch the road. Everyone looked at the car. Sitting with Al in his XK 120 was real hot stuff — we were the center of attraction. How could a milkman afford a Jaguar? Answer: working seven days a week from dawn to dusk and taking off one week a year to go to the annual Indianapolis car race.

In 1953, I was eligible to take my driving test about ten days after my 16th birthday. Though I knew how to drive, I was still very nervous on the highway. I don't recall any written exam at that time and there also weren't any driving schools or driving instructors.

I learned to drive first, as did Dale, in a WWII army surplus jeep. In Dale's case, it belonged to her father; in my case, it belonged to the father of my friend, Skippy Greenman. I had road practice with my father when we went on house calls together. He was not a patient teacher and was often critical. If I did something wrong, he'd cry out, "What in the world did you do that for?"

My response would be a meek "I don't know."

I knew exactly what I wanted for my first car — a 1928 Model A Ford Roadster with a rumble seat. Al helped me search the countryside for one, mostly by word of mouth. We looked in other people's barns or garages or asked everyone we saw if they knew anyone who had a Model A Ford. When we eventually found one, it cost $75. A bargain! I made seven dollars per day at the time so I had to work just over ten days to save up for it. The price, of course, didn't include the time and money it would take to make it roadworthy.

My friend Tommy Griffin's father owned a body shop. I went to him for advice on how to repaint my car. Tommy's father agreed to help, but I had to do all the sanding myself, by hand. He would bang out the dents and respray the car. It was a beauty. I painted it two-tone green — light green on the body and dark green on the mudguards. I was very proud of this car. Driving it made me feel special because it drew people's attention, not unlike Al's Jaguar.

One of my very first passengers was Patty Smith, Dale's best friend from childhood. I also took my mother for a ride and, of course, my father wanted to drive it. At the time, his car was a Porsche. I don't think he was too impressed, but he was happy for me, nonetheless.

My working relationship with Al and his family ended when I went away to prep school. Before leaving America in 1968, I visited Al after not having seen him during my eight years away from home at prep school and college. He had finally gotten married and had two grown daughters, both graduate nurses, living their own lives, one in Maine, the other in Georgia. Al's mother and father had died. He had sold the farm, but continued to drive the Flying Eagle bus and had taken up driving a local yellow school bus. On another visit a few years later, Al seemed old for the first time. He had fallen off his tractor while plowing the office driveway of the local newspaper. His wife told me that he had plowed that same driveway since he graduated from the local high school at the age of 17. He was probably 75 then.

That same afternoon, I contacted the editor and owner of the local newspaper and suggested that there might be a human-interest story in Al Boyson. He arranged for an interview. Two years later, on another visit, Al showed me the article and we both got very teary. By that time, his wife had died of a stroke and he was living alone in the house he'd bought and paid for in full when they'd married 35 years earlier. "I don't buy what I can't pay for," he used to say. I often heard him say about people: "the bank lets him drive their car" or "the bank lets him sleep in their house." He probably felt a little resentful when someone who was behind on a milk bill payment had a brand new car in the driveway.

Sometime later, I received a letter from his daughter in Maine. She wrote that Al had died and had been laid to rest beside his wife in the local cemetery, overlooking Hawley Pond. It was the same pond where my father taught me to ice skate in the winter and where Al taught me to catch bullfrogs, which we used to sell at the local upscale restaurant. I'm not sure frogs' legs were even on the menu, but the owner bought them and seemed delighted at having done so.

K Through 12

I started school at the age of six. It was the beginning of years and years of torment. I struggled in every subject from the first day. Not one subject became any easier over the next twenty-two years. I couldn't memorize things like everybody else.

I worried constantly about upcoming tests or that I would be called upon to do a recitation or go to the blackboard. I grappled with multiplication tables. I would often get teary-eyed when I failed. I had butterflies in my stomach when faced with the simplest academic subject, and I had chronic headaches from the time I was 7 until the age of 26. Thank goodness for aspirin. It was only after Herculean efforts, extra study time, and special training that I learned to read, but even then, very badly. Even now, I get around it by avoiding reading aloud. I won't sing out loud in church; I'm always two lines behind the rest of the congregation.

Primary School

Osteomyelitis kept me in the hospital for many months of my second and third years of school. Because of my inability to catch up on basic lessons, I repeated the third grade. That was a decision made by the school and agreed to by my parents. I was deeply hurt at being left behind. But at my age, my parents knew best. They knew it would be senseless for me to continue to the next grade. I was, of course, very ashamed.

Repeating the third grade did not really help. I was simply making the same mistakes over again. I would, however, be moved into the next grade and the following one. Where nature failed to provide me with a scholastic aptitude, it did provide me with a phenomenal level of energy, an insatiable need to succeed and a sense of ambition. This gave me an incredible willingness to make an effort. Fortunately, my father recognized these qualities in me and with his help, I obtained an education. He was always supportive. Concerns were expressed in a positive manner; the idea of leaving school was never discussed.

In spite of my academic failings, I still enjoyed going to school. I was popular with my friends and good at organized playground activities. I don't recall being teased or bullied because of my handicap.

Miss Hayes, my teacher, made me do my multiplication tables while the other students went to the playground. She believed that multiplication tables were more important than recess. I understood her rationale — I wasn't resentful nor did I feel I was being punished. I knew she was trying to help, but I couldn't help feeling disheartened. Everyone remembers an outstanding teacher like Miss Hayes. I wish I had a chance to thank her today, to show my appreciation for inspiring the desire to learn in me.

Eventually, I made it to the fourth grade. I remember it being a wonderful year. There was a classroom shortage at the local high school across the road from where we lived. This forced the school board to reopen some old one-room schools throughout the various boroughs of Newtown.

I attended one of these turn-of-the-century schools that year. They were scattered throughout the various boroughs of Newtown and were built to a standard configuration. Ours was called Lands End School, situated in the Lands End Borough on half an acre of land. Firewood was stacked in an orderly pile at one side of the front door, for use in the potbelly stove in the center of the schoolhouse. Near the roadway was a standing water pump and at the far side of the playground was an outhouse with two doors — one for boys and one for girls. In the outhouse were two heavy planks with two holes on which to sit. On a rotating basis, the students would pour lye down one of the two holes. We were never sure exactly why we had to do this except for a vague understanding that while the lye was working on the one hole we were meant to use the other.

Miss Heller was the teacher at Lands End School. In contrast to Miss Hayes, she was young, slim, tall, and very beautiful. From that day forward, all of my girlfriends, with few exceptions, would be tall, slim, and beautiful.

I had my first serious girlfriend that year, at the age of 12. Her name was Eileen Craig. I thought she was so pretty and the fact that she liked me more than she liked the other students made me feel proud. We exchanged photos as a sign of true affection. I remember I had my photo taken in my new navy blue pea jacket. It was the must-have jacket at the time and I hounded my parents until they bought me one. I gave Eileen my ID bracelet to wear as a further token of my affection.

At the same time, I was in love with Miss Heller and I thought she liked me, too. I knew she favored me and gave me more attention than the other students. I said things that made her smile. My desk was placed next to the potbelly stove — a sort of recognition or status. To this day, I remember how Miss Heller would pass by me as she walked between the rows of desks. Her silk skirt would sometimes touch my desk, her hips just above my eyes. I could smell her perfume. I wanted to tell her how beautiful she looked. When she left for home at the end of each day, I would watch her hike up her skirt just above the knee as she got into her car — a 1947 Ford coupe sedan. If I had been older, she would have been my Mrs. Robinson.

I liked being in a one-room schoolhouse because it felt more like going to school, rather than simply going across the street from our house to the high school. I enjoyed the 20-minute ride in those huge yellow buses. There was no playground equipment such as swings and seesaws, just open pasture. We played all kinds of games there: kickball, stickball, softball, tag, and marbles. All of our "athletic equipment" had to be carried inside at the end of recess.

Miss Heller's comments in my report card generally said something along the lines of, "He pays close attention, he is popular with his classmates, he tries very hard, he seems to be making some progress..." and the like. But my grades were terrible. My father knew that something needed to be done. I was 12 years old and I could barely read, write, spell, or do math. When we went on his calls together, he always stopped at the post office to collect his mail along with the New York Herald Tribune. He would ask me to read the headlines on the various news items on the first page. He could see that I could hardly read. I was sad and embarrassed.

I recently read an interview in The Sunday Times about Jackie Stewart, the world champion Formula One driver. "I was so poor at school and told so often that I was stupid or lazy that I came to believe it myself," he said. "In fact, I was dyslexic. You don't cure that; you get around it."

The key phrase in his comment is "you get around it." You use only the words you can spell; you avoid reading, and you use your fingers to do math. I figured out how to get around it when I was young by being keen, sociable, and responsive to adults. More than anything else, adults like to see spontaneity in children; they want to see a reaction. That I could do. I never believed I was lazy, but I certainly believed I was dumb.

Sometimes my father would lose his patience with me, scolding me for not doing better at school. But I don't remember him ever accusing me of being lazy or dumb. It was important to him that I succeed academically and I absorbed that. He never actually helped me in my efforts to read. He started his day early and ended it late. In hindsight, perhaps he should have been teaching me how to read and write instead of playing table pool with me between the hours of nine and ten at night.

In fifth grade, at the age of 12, my father heard about a teacher who lived 45 minutes away by bus on the other side of Derby (often referred to as the armpit of Connecticut). Mrs. Rosin gave remedial reading lessons. It was arranged for me to leave school early on three afternoons every week and travel by the Flying Eagle Bus Service to her house. At the time, she offered a glimmer of hope. It was the first time I got off the terrible treadmill of trying and actually started to learn how to read and spell. It was, however, only a start.

"David," she said, "if you can spell house and you can say your alphabet, then you can learn to spell mouse." She taught me the sound of words by breaking them up and sounding out the syllables. I began to catch on.

Rumsey Hall

Before going off to Rumsey Hall School at the age of 13, Newtown, Connecticut, was my world. I thought I was living life to the fullest, all within a radius of five miles. But then my life exploded — I went places, I saw things, I had experiences I had never imagined. I came into other people's lives and they in turn came into mine with an intimacy that I could never have conceived of before. At 12, I set out on an adventure that would last another 55 years. Rumsey Hall School was just the start. It was time to become *me*, and being sent away to school was something positive. I felt enthusiastic, encouraged, and supportive of the school itself. On the other hand, many students were sent there because of family issues: divorce, parental careers, single parent situations, and behavioral problems.

As my father, mother, and I unpacked the car and brought my things to the dormitory room, I met my roommate, Tyler Day. I immediately realized that he would not be a friend. He was tense, loud, affected, and ill at ease with himself. He had been at Rumsey Hall since he was seven. He knew too much. I preferred to have another new boy, one, like me, who was also a little scared and timid.

The dormitory was composed of seven double rooms, each with a bunk bed. I was keen to have the top bunk, which I got, but I later learned that Tyler took it upon himself to change my nameplate from the bottom bed to the top because he wanted the bottom for himself. Old boys knew to arrive early: He who gets there first, gets the best pick of locker, bed, and other little amenities.

Our housemaster, Mr. Pavock, lived on the ground floor with his wife and two children. He introduced himself to my parents, showed us the room, and described life in a dormitory. He made it clear that everyone would be expected to participate in athletic activities. Those who could not or simply did not want to were assigned to team projects, such as gardening, ground work, or forestry maintenance. They were disparagingly referred to as "the work squad." As the emphasis in the school was on competitiveness in scholarship and athletics, I felt sorry for those who could not participate. I considered myself lucky — I was well-coordinated and enjoyed sports although I was only an average player. I was good at ice hockey, my favorite sport. It never occurred to me that "the work squad" might have felt sorry for us poor fools getting banged around in the freezing snow or running after some silly ball.

I was introduced to a completely foreign world in this new school. The students and their backgrounds seemed so different from mine. I suppose I thought that the rest of the world was just like home. I thought all my new friends would be just like Skippy, Teddy, and Terry in Newtown. I was fascinated by the other students' lives. It seemed incredible that they lived in apartments in New York City or that their fathers had chauffeurs or they actually lived in Florida all the time — I thought places like Florida were only for visiting. I was aware of being different from them, of my own persona. I lived in the country, I had my own rifle and shot squirrels and groundhogs; I drove a tractor and cycled wherever I wanted. This made me different from them, but then I may have been as foreign to them as they were to me.

I didn't get homesick until the second week at school, when we were allowed to make our first Sunday night telephone call to our families. I tried to hide the fact that I was crying while talking to my mother. I'm sure she also felt sad.

The first time we were permitted to go home was at the end of November, over the Thanksgiving holiday. After that, parents were allowed to visit the campus on weekends and could take their children off-campus for Sunday lunch after the church service. My parents rarely came, and I preferred it that way. Short visits were more painful. Putting a time limit on seeing your parents seemed unnatural somehow.

The day before going home for Thanksgiving break was tremendously exciting. Everyone was very anxious and expectant about going home for his/her first holiday. The train picked us up at New Milford, Connecticut, having made a special stop on its regular route to New York City. I got off at Danbury, where my mother met me. I got very teary, as did she. We didn't wear a school uniform except on special occasions: parents' day, church, or leaving the school campus. We wore a dark blue blazer, a white shirt, the school tie, and light grey flannel trousers. The blazer had the school emblem on its breast pocket. I felt rather proud meeting my mother dressed like that. She had never seen me as a young man before, wearing a tie and jacket. I felt more grown up than I ever had.

I was the first of my gang to go to boarding school and on my return, I was keen to tell them about my new experiences. I soon became aware that they were not particularly interested. It was my first hint that we were growing apart.

I went on the milk route with Al and saw all the people I knew. I think Al was proud to be taking me around. He shouted out loud to people I knew: "Hey — look at Doc (my nickname), back from the fancy boarding school." I felt more welcome on the milk route than with my old gang.

Being a new boy in school for the first time (there would be other times in other schools) was an experience I carried with me for the rest of my life. I could not believe that we would be taking Latin and French classes and waking up every morning to put on a tie and jacket. There was no mother reminding you to brush your teeth or seeing that your shirt was tucked in or that you'd been wearing the same pair of socks for a week. And, the idea of calling all the teachers "Sir" was very new to me.

Instinctively, I knew it was important to fit in and get along. The phrase "He seems to be fitting in well" was a compliment for me. At the time, approval was essential to me. One way to fit in was to keep your head down and watch what others were doing. A faster way of gaining recognition was by being a good athlete, which helped me very much.

I was a good athlete, but not good enough to deserve recognition, at least not until the ice hockey season started. I had an unusual bicycle that helped a little in the first few weeks. I had painted it chartreuse green and fashioned a dual exhaust. It had saddlebags, an aerial with a raccoon tail, and a leopard-skin seat made for me by one of our milk route customers who owned an upholstery company. During the first few weeks of school, the bicycle provided me with a certain distinction. That it didn't derive from competitiveness soon turned it into a curiosity.

I hadn't yet established any close friendships, so during my free time, I wandered around like a dog sniffing for new territory. I looked at different classrooms, wandered down to the field house, or played catch with anyone who had a baseball. I wanted to remain a little aloof; I didn't yet want to be identified with any particular group.

One day, I was walking along one of the buildings, going no place in particular, when I passed a large lounge room where some older students were playing table pool. Timid but curious, I ventured in. It was full of the older senior boys. They stopped talking for a moment and looked in my direction. They said nothing, so I just watched. They left the room when they finished playing.

On another occasion, I stopped by and watched again. After they left, I put a few balls on the table and started to do some practice shots. I did the same a few days later when Archie Peck — tall, thin, popular, and an excellent athlete — passed by and watched me play. When I missed one of the shots, he simply took his turn and when he missed, which he did almost immediately, I continued. That was my break. I established myself as a good pool player and soon picked up the name "The Edge." A nickname was an immediate sign of acceptance or ridicule. Luckily, in my case it was the former. Those hours spent playing pool with my father on a professional-sized pool table in the basement of our house had paid off.

My father treated every new hobby with great enthusiasm and insisted on purchasing all the paraphernalia connected with it. He got interested in sailing and bought a boat; he got interested in trap shooting and helped start a gun club; he turned to cabinet making and immediately converted part of our cellar into a complete woodworking shop. He started using silver in jewelry making and to this day, Dale wears one of his necklaces. So, when he got interested in playing pool, it was not unusual to find a pool table being delivered to our house. Naturally, he wanted someone to play against. He made a stepping stool that I could easily carry around from one side of the table to the other, and we would play together after he finished work.

My mother would shout down from the top of the basement stairs: "Benton, for goodness sake, let the boy go to bed. It's nearly ten o'clock and he has school tomorrow."

"I'll send him up right away," said my father, but he would always wait until the second shout from the top of the stairs. Then he would smile at me and say, "I guess you'd better go up." By the time I presented myself to the lounge at Rumsey Hall, I wasn't a bad player. The seniors organized a school-wide tournament. I came in second.

My greatest anxiety as a new boy at Rumsey Hall was undressing in front of others. I was nervous about how I would compare to other naked boys. As part of our orientation to the school, Mr. Pavock showed the new boys the field house where we were expected to shower after athletics. The shower room itself was quite large, with ten showerheads sticking out along three walls. A long window stretched along the top of two of the walls. The floor was polished concrete and the walls were covered with dark grey tiles. It looked like some sort of torture chamber. I dreaded the thought that one day soon I would have to shower naked with ten other boys.

Every Saturday night, all the boys in the school were supposed to take a shower and stand for inspection, naked, in front of the weekend duty officer. He would sit in a chair with a clipboard. Beside him was an empty chair where we put one foot at a time so he could inspect between our toes, make sure our toenails were cut, and that we didn't have athletes' foot. This way, parents would know that their little boys were clean at least once a week. For the record, I never witnessed any unconventional behavior by the inspecting teacher. Nor do I recall any teacher actually touching us. I don't think the boys in my class were aware of situations that might imply homosexuality (that, unfortunately, would come the following year).

The shower room experience was not as traumatic as I had anticipated and neither was the weekly inspection. But I do remember how relieved I was that my penis was not the shortest one. Still, I saw others that were clearly larger; I wished mine was slightly more "formidable." I went through the rest of my life confident that I was of average size. Dale told me that young girls felt the same way about their breasts.

In my last year at the school, at the age of 15, the shower room went from being a source of possible threat to a favorite pastime. Three of the ten showers did not have proper showerheads. Instead of coming out in a spray, the water flowed in a steady stream from a height of six feet. We would cup our penises in one hand and allow the water to stream on it while adjusting the speed of the water and temperature with the other until we came to orgasm. Most of us could not ejaculate so there was no fear of slippery floors. In spite of the wide and varied education that Al Boyson provided, and despite my interest in the opposite sex, masturbation was a completely new phenomenon. I remember my first night at school. Just before falling asleep, I felt a slight movement of the bed and heavy breathing from the lower bunk. I asked Tyler Day if he was okay.

"Yes," he said, "I'm fine."

"Why are you crying?" I asked. He started laughing and explained to me exactly what he was doing. Because I didn't like him, I assumed that the practice was associated with unlikeable people. After a few weeks, Mr. Pavock, to his credit, was sympathetic to my "roommate situation" and arranged for me to move in with a classmate, Bill Adam, who had become a friend. When I realized that he, too, was doing the same thing as Tyler Day, I assumed that everyone did it and that it was probably all right, although I knew instinctively that it wasn't.

I don't believe we had any guilty feelings about masturbation and on occasion, we would have a collective session, where one boy would read aloud from a dirty book. To this day, I remember one phrase: "He toyed with her breast." I thought it was real literary prose. A few ejaculated half a teaspoon, others a few drops, and still others, such as me, did not ejaculate at all.

Most of us had at least one trouser pocket with a hole so we could easily masturbate whenever we liked. In study hall sessions, practice was required to avoid any obvious movement in the trouser or unusual breathing. Your eyes had to remain fixed on the raised desk of the study hall master.

There was only one lavatory room for the study hall area. Without ventilation, it constantly stank. I hated it. More often than not the toilets didn't work or were stopped up; the turds of the previous student floated in a near-overflowing bowl of yellow water. Just entering the room filled me with terror. But we never complained about it. As long as possible, I waited until the dining room opened or ran back to our dorm lavatory.

On one occasion, I had no other option. Thankfully, I was the only one using the lavatory at the time. But then, as I sat on the toilet in one of the doorless stalls, someone came into the room. I heard him walking slowly toward me. Staring at the floor was the only way to preserve a little privacy.

Into my line of sight stepped the wingtips of senior student Thomas Van Wolf. He was heavyset and always wore a dark suit instead of a sports jacket and trousers like the rest of us. No one dared to call him Tom or Tommy. To a visitor, this starchy dresser with his large ostentatious gold cufflinks could easily have passed for a young teacher rather than a student. He spoke only in words of two or more syllables. He was arrogant — he bullied others with his intellectual arrogance and physical maturity; he was a big guy. As he stood there in front of me, I continued to stare at the floor.

"Look at me, Egee, look up," he said. I knew I was in trouble. With a fierce pull of his zipper he laid his large penis across his hand and shouted: "Suck on it, you little bastard, suck on it."

I immediately shouted. "No, no, no!" I put my head in my lap. He laughed at me and walked away. I remember every single detail of that experience. At some point, I walked back to my room feeling lonely and intimidated while gradually recovering from the shock. I got up on my bed, put my face to the wall and started to cry again. I could not talk to anyone about it — not even close friends or my roommate. What if they just laughed at my embarrassment and humiliation? I definitely could not speak to the teachers because Van Wolf would know I had squealed on him. He would have made my life miserable, and I didn't want to be forced to leave the school. How many other boys got the same treatment? How many others like me were too scared to speak up for fear of reprisal? There were no whistle-blowers in those days.

I was too embarrassed to tell Mr. Pavock. Looked at from a slightly different angle, nothing had actually happened. But it was still a nightmare. I wonder if anything comparable happens in girls' schools. I can now understand better how priests were able to abuse young boys and go undetected. We were afraid to speak up.

Boarding school had its dark sides, but on the whole, I enjoyed it immensely. Classes at Rumsey Hall were small, usually no more than ten to twelve students, ensuring lots of individual attention. Although the school was organized according to class year, the classroom work was flexible. Grades depended on individual ability. Because I had difficulty reading, I was put in a class with others who had the same problem. As I was new to Latin and French, I was put with similar students. Extra classes were taken as appropriate. But despite the extra help and the flexible structure, I still found the academic aspects of school a constant struggle. However, my determination and continued efforts to understand classroom work convinced my teachers to give me extra help.

One teacher I've remembered all my life is Mr. Wishart. I don't remember his first name because we always called our teachers by their last names, with "Mr." in front. Mr. Wishart taught history and English. Although elusive and distant, he commanded respect by not overstepping the teacher-student boundary lines, and not playing favorites. But he was genuinely interested in us as students. When he spoke, he spoke softly and we listened. In my mind, his classic preppy attire reinforced my sister Elaine's style.

Mr. Wishart was responsible for arranging the school's poetry reading competition. The winners — one from the lower school and one from the upper school — recited a poem at the annual graduation ceremony. Mr. Wishart had to approve the poems we recited. Most students selected poems from something in the school library — usually something we had studied, something standard. I saw a poem in the Saturday Evening Post. It compared a man arranging a luncheon meeting over the phone and a woman doing the same. Although very sexist in today's terms, it was funny and compared to the others, relatively short. Mr. Wishart found it wonderful and was impressed by my ability to memorize it. Why I couldn't do that with multiplication, I don't know.

The poem was such a great success — I won! I knew Mr. Wishart was proud of me. At my graduation the following year, I told my father that I'd like to give Mr. Wishart a Sheaffer fountain pen. I explained to him what an important teacher he had been to me. My father was very sympathetic. I was slightly nervous when I presented it to Mr. Wishart, but I know he was pleased to receive it. I never saw him again after that. I learned that he had left the school to become the headmaster of a school in Pennsylvania. In my later years, I'm sorry I was never able to tell him how important he was to me and how much I admired him as a teacher.

At the end of my first year at Rumsey Hall, I felt more at ease than I ever had in my whole life, in spite of the constant anxiety about my academic work. Boarding school suited me. I don't think it ruined me or warped me the way English boarding schools are supposed to; I was fitting in very well. I was as happy at school as I was at home. I knew this was an unusual situation because most boys seemed to come from some sort of dysfunctional family situation. My roommate Bill and I seemed to be among the few who came from normal families. I don't think the school had any scholarship programs; I believe all of the other students came from upper-middle-class or rich families. For example, one boy was the son of the then president of Chile.

During school holidays, I used to visit my friends at their homes. Bill Adam lived in Torrington, Connecticut. His parents had a vacation house on a lake. They had a water skiing boat, and it was with them that I learned how to water ski. Other times, I visited my friend Jay Gerli. His parents were divorced, but lived near each other in Greenwich, Connecticut. Jay's father had a big greenhouse where he grew orchids as a hobby. He had a six-car garage and a chauffeur. I remember Jay's father being chauffeured around in a black 1943 Buick sedan. I also visited Godfrey Redman's family, which was really something because they were the wealthiest people I'd ever met. They had a huge house, many servants, two swimming pools, and a reflecting pool. Godfrey's mother was very nice; I liked her. She patiently explained to me the purpose of a reflection pool and showed me how to view it. She gave us her attention and asked us questions. It's nice when an adult seems interested in what a young person thinks about something. We used to go to the window that overlooked one of the two swimming pools and watch his mother and her friends swimming naked together and then we would go into the bathhouse and examine their underwear.

As part of the indoctrination into Rumsey Hall, every student was assigned one of two colors, blue or red (which had nothing to do with one's politics). Your assigned color remained with you throughout your time at Rumsey Hall. Many of the activities were broken down according to these two teams. This also applied to all sporting and academic endeavors. I was a Blue; Tyler was a Red.

At the beginning of my second year at Rumsey Hall, the Blues elected me as their president of the upper forms.[1] As president, I was permitted to pick my own committee members. The appointments needed to be approved by Dr. Sherry, the director of the school. Among the Blues was Jerry Miller. He was in the fourth form. His older brother, Peter, was also in our class. Jerry was a real troublemaker. He wasn't a bully like Van Wolf, nor was he destructive. He could probably be best described as mischievous. If someone jumped out of a third-story window into a snow bank, it was Jerry Miller. If someone rang the school bell at an unusual hour or if the flag was flying upside down, these incidents were probably caused by Jerry Miller. I was amused by him and liked his spirit. He did well in his studies and had a good attitude on the field. But he was a pain. I decided that the best way to deal with Jerry was to get him on my side. So I appointed him the Blues' vice-president.

---

1   In private schools, the term *Form* was used to denote grade. In prep school, fifth form equaled 12th grade, fourth form 11th grade, etc..

I had remembered hearing my father talk to Mr. Cap Legros, principal of the local high school in Newtown. They were talking about troublesome children in the classroom and on the playground. I remembered only snippets of the conversation: "If you can include the child ... try to make him feel responsible, give him something to do."

The school director quizzed me after I had selected Jerry. I think he was rather impressed with what I was trying to do. Sometimes, teachers would pass me and ask: "How are you getting along with your new vice-president, Egee?" There was a generally positive feeling about it and I must say, Jerry surprised everyone by his attitude.

In June 1952, it was time for me to leave Rumsey Hall. I received a conditional acceptance to Loomis School, a very good prep school with an excellent reputation as a feeder school for the Ivy League colleges. The condition was to attend their six-week summer school session. Little did I know then that I would spend the next four years going to school twelve months a year.

At the graduation ceremony, various awards were handed out, both athletic and academic. I excelled at neither. There were also the best-effort and the achievement awards. But the most sought after was the Headmaster's Cup, which was presented to the best all-around student who "illustrated the ideals of the school." I was very proud that my name appeared in my hometown's local newspaper as the winner.

Loomis

I was going from a school of approximately 100 students to a school of 550. When I went for a visit, I was overwhelmed by its size. It never occurred to me to ask my father if I could go to a smaller school. At that age, like most children, I went where my father told me to go.

It was a hot summer's day when he drove me to Danbury and put me on a bus going to Windsor, Connecticut, with a suitcase packed with enough clothes for six weeks. The bus dropped me at the Windsor depot. I discovered that it was about a three-mile walk to the school. With a convincing look of vulnerability, I was able to find a nice lady who agreed to drive me to the school. As we drove through the gates, I saw the same huge brick building I had visited a few months earlier. This time its large front door was closed and there was nobody around. I shoved the door open, dragging my suitcase inside. The door slammed shut, echoing off the walls of an empty corridor. I wandered down the hall; I couldn't believe it. Not a soul was in sight. The high ceilings and wide corridor made it look even more desolate. I turned around and walked down another corridor. I heard footsteps coming from around the corner and there, like magic, was the popular Archie Peck from Rumsey Hall.

"The Edge!" he shouted. "My god, what are you doing here?" We chatted a bit, and then went off to see if there was anybody else around.

The summer school was informally run. There were roughly 50 students in a school built to accommodate more than ten times as many. It was all but closed down. There were a few classrooms in operation. There were teachers about, but they were only available to give instruction during the classes. The only organized activity seemed to be three meals a day, served in a huge dining room. We were tucked into a small corner of the room.

There was another building with a Tuck Shop,[2] run by the students, with Archie as the head volunteer. He was also responsible for assigning work hours. If you worked in the Tuck Shop — the solitary social gathering point was considered a privilege — you were "in." Archie arranged it for me.

I was unaccustomed to this much freedom — the complete lack of supervision or organized activities. When you studied, how you studied, where you studied, and what you did with

---

2   In Eastern boarding schools, Tuck Shops sell candy bars to students after lunch.

your spare time were entirely up to you. There were only three rules: attend classes; remain on the Loomis School campus; and if you must go to the village, go with another student. Other than that, you were under house arrest for six weeks.

That was the first time in my life that I actually read several books on my own initiative — real books, 200 pages long, with hard covers and no pictures. I would go to my room in the heat of the afternoon, lie sideways on my bed, put my feet up on the wall and read *The Catcher in the Rye* or *The Grapes of Wrath*.

I took the experiences of all the characters in the stories very personally and worried about what would happen if these same things happened to me. Reading Upton Sinclair's *The Jungle* had a profound effect on me. I never imagined that reading a book could evoke such an emotional response. I felt anger towards those responsible for corrupt and abusive business practices and sorrow for the conditions workers were forced to endure.

I believed that if someone was bad, they deserved the punishment of poverty; but, if they were essentially a good person, worked hard and followed the rules, everything would be alright. You may not be rich (like I thought my parents were), but you could certainly have a good life — as good as Al Boyson, Stretch Forbell (the phone company lineman), or my grandfather, who worked as a machinist with no education. They all had modest incomes, but they seemed happy. However, in the books I read, with the exception of The Catcher in the Rye, characters were punished for their poverty. Perhaps I was feeling sorry for myself — my poverty was the inability to succeed academically.

Up to this point, I had never really experienced loneliness. Now I was consumed by it. I had no real company except during classroom periods. I thought I was living in an empty world with empty buildings, empty playing fields, empty car parks, an empty quadrangle — I walked endlessly through dimly-lit dormitory corridors and classrooms with no one in them. At least, I had the big shower room all to myself. Of course, there were others, but the place was so big, and since everybody was taking such diverse courses, the impression of solitude, isolation, and friendlessness was overwhelming.

When the regular academic year began, I was considered only partly a new boy when in fact all I knew about the school was empty buildings. I was coming from a pre-prep school and had a slight advantage over the other new students for a brief period of time. At Rumsey Hall, I'd had an introduction to some of the classes — such as French, Latin, and Algebra — so the first three months of the school year were really a review period for me. I was able to manage satisfactorily. But the rest of the class would soon catch up and pass me by.

The housemaster of the freshman dormitory was Mr. Haller. I recall him as a good and fair man. He would scold students if they deserved it, and he would praise them when they did something good. He wasn't particularly friendly, but he wasn't unfriendly, either. Part of his job was to make sure our rooms were neat and tidy. There weren't any regular inspection days as at Rumsey Hall. Mr. Haller would casually look into your room at any time. He'd knock first and if we were in class, he was free to look about our rooms. I had a bad habit of putting my dirty socks in the rain gutters that ran just below our dormitory window in a mansard roof. (The mansard roof would enter my life again at a later date.) I got away with this for a while until it rained one night and my dirty socks stopped up the drain. I thought it was a brilliant idea that the rain would wash my socks and I wouldn't have to bother. Of course, the maintenance people had to be called to sort out the problem. Mr. Haller knew my socks had caused the problem. When it happened a second time, he gave me my first good scolding. For some inexplicable reason, and to this day I don't know why, I continued to do this habitually because the gutter seemed so convenient and the mansard roof made it so easy.

Mr. Haller walked with a serious limp and so had a clearly distinguishable way of moving around. Sitting in the study hall,

I heard his particular walk coming down the aisle between the desks. I instinctively knew that he was coming to mine. He stopped, held up a pair of my socks between his thumb and index finger, and then let them drop on the desk. "Bring them with you," he said, and walked away. I followed him. I was never beaten or abused, but that day I got the worst reprimand I have ever received. He literally screamed at me. He kept asking if I was retarded: "Why do you misbehave in this way? Why? *Why?*" I was in tears when he excused me to my room.

I was miserable, probably traumatized. No one had ever spoken to me that way. My father would spank us, but he never talked to us in such a manner. Perhaps Mr. Haller wanted to spank me, but couldn't because of school rules. Maybe I subconsciously wanted to be thrown out of the school, though I didn't particularly dislike it at a conscious level. I was falling further and further behind in my classes and despite my best efforts, the headmaster decided that Loomis was not for me. My father came to the school and had a long discussion with the headmaster. He didn't tell me that I wouldn't be coming back — nor did anyone else, until I took my final exams for the year.

Bridgeport University

My father must have learned something as a result of the rather lengthy meeting with the headmaster at Loomis School, because it was only a few weeks later that I was back in summer school, this time in a special program at the University of Bridgeport, which lasted one month. I don't recall the term dyslexia being used — the terms "remedial studies" and specifically "remedial reading" were more popular at the time.

Headed by one of the largest ladies I would ever meet, Gladys Parsons, Bridgeport University was one of the earliest centers for remedial studies. She was exceedingly stout — very big and very tall. I liked her, and she seemed interested in me as a student — or perhaps as a challenge. She was also the only woman I had ever met with the same name as my mother. The summer program was a condensed version of the year-long program set up for the benefit of the university students. After the summer session, I remained there for the entire academic year. Through an agreement with Miss Parsons, I was entered as a "special student" and took only the remedial studies. During the next eleven months, I would hopefully, finally, learn to read and comprehend. At the time, I was 16.

Unbelievable as it may seem, I saw my old friend Archie Peck at the university on two occasions. We were in different classes, but he was on the same summer program. However, it was more of an acknowledgement than a reunion. I had a feeling he was a little embarrassed — he didn't want to be seen following in my footsteps. Archie was older than me, which made me feel sorrier for him than for myself. There was some comfort in the knowledge that someone I had admired had a similar problem as mine. That feeling does not work in reverse.

After years at boarding school, with holidays spent at friends' homes, being back with my family for an entire year was a novel experience and felt like a reentry. My old friends in Newtown had been sent to boarding school, and I had drifted apart from the ones that stayed at the local school. That year, my friends were mostly my parents and their friends. As I was now able to drive, I also visited friends in other locations. When I wasn't studying, I continued to keep my father company on his house calls as I had done four years earlier. We went not only on house calls, but also on public health inspections at restaurants and bars, interviews at the state mental hospital, and accidents and autopsies. My father was the state medical officer for our county; therefore, his medical responsibilities extended beyond patient care.

That year, I lived in the guest accommodations that were built into the attic of the house. The attic was my refuge. I would study there and I would lie in bed staring at the ceiling, daydreaming about what I was going to do when I grew up and was able to read. My father was aware of my unhappiness, but we both knew without saying it that I would stick to it and do what was required.

I had this vague idea that once I got through school, I would go on to university. I was envious of those who were able to absorb school material and understand it almost without effort. Why was schooling such a chore for me? Why was algebra impossible for me to comprehend? It was like a part of my brain was missing — the part that had to do with school learning just wasn't there.

There were a number of techniques that were used to improve students' reading and comprehension levels. The only one I specifically remember was the use of an overhead projector. We were placed in a darkened room and a series of numbers were briefly projected on the screen. We then had to write the numbers down in the same series as projected. The numbers appeared for shorter and shorter periods of time and the series got longer and longer. Did it improve my reading skills? I suppose so. There were other courses related to spelling and math. Was I better at those subjects? Maybe. But I was still aware that I was at the bottom of the class. Mrs. Parsons did what she could, but I would still continue being pushed to the next class, as I had been all my life.

After an entire school year, I left Bridgeport and was conditionally accepted to Wooster School in Danbury, Connecticut. The condition was, once again, that I take two afternoon courses before the regular academic year started. But this time, God looked down on me, smiled, and said, "David, this is *your* year."

Wooster

I entered Wooster School for the eleventh and twelfth years of my education, which also included two years of summer school sessions. In the interview before acceptance, I met with the headmaster, Reverend John Verdery. He put me at ease immediately. The conversation flowed easily and I had a feeling it was going well. I was enthusiastic about the school at the end of the meeting and over the next two years, I came to appreciate the help that he offered me.

My father thought that since my younger brother John never had a private school experience and had much less trouble in basic learning, it would be good for him to attend, too. John, however, did not enjoy life at a private school. He was ill at ease among the other students, and he did not enjoy being away from home. He wasn't interested in athletics or the school community, in general. He left after his first year to finish at the local high school in Newtown.

While my father viewed Wooster School as a school of last resort, it was the best environment for me to continue to grow and mature. Though it was only a 15-minute drive from our home, my father knew that I would prefer being a boarder than a day student. It was a small school with a total student body of only 150 students, with about 18 of them being in my class. Getting through Wooster School was an academic struggle, but I was at least able to read, write, and comprehend some of what I read. I still found it difficult to do well in other classes — chemistry, physics, and geometry were impossible for me. I would have to repeat these classes in summer school sessions or replace them with softer subjects.

Wooster School prided itself on having a "self-help" program. All the students were assigned daily chores. Members of the senior class, including me, were assigned different areas of responsibilities to ensure that these chores were carried out. Some students had to set up the dining room before each meal and clear up afterwards; others worked on dishwashing duties. (Kitchen duties were favored — we could scavenge for extra food.) Other students had to ensure that the dormitories were kept tidy and clean. I was appointed school postman, which included occasional babysitting assignments for the headmaster's three children in the evening, and the mail of the headmaster's wife being personally delivered to their campus home. It was the least popular job because it was one of the few duties that didn't require supervising others. The responsibilities were also about status: the assignments were a measure of a particular senior's place within the class. Prefects and dining room heads had the highest status.

Anticipating my possible disappointment, the headmaster called me to his office and explained why I was selected. He said he had a personal interest in the assignment because the individual concerned had to be able to interact with his wife and children. During my first year, I had secretly fallen in love with his wife, Sue, so I didn't object to the assignment at all. Sue was very outgoing and had a wonderfully low, almost masculine, laugh. She was blonde with an East Coast manner. She dressed in a preppy style, which was important to me then. I thought she was wonderful. Whenever she asked if I would mind babysitting, I agreed immediately.

John Verdery laid out the rules on the first night: "The children will be in bed, so unless you hear anything, I don't think you'll have to worry. You can use my study and you are welcome to use the record player and the bar, but don't abuse it." On the way out, Sue always told me that I could help myself to anything from the fridge so long as I didn't eat the next day's lunch.

I babysat once or twice a month. On occasion, I would drive Sue into Danbury. Once I had to take her to New York City to pick up a new Peugeot station wagon they had purchased. We drove to New York in her old car and she drove the new one back.

We were eating lunch in New York before our return trip when I said, "Mrs. Verdery, when I'm ready, I'm going to marry someone just like you."

"Really? Why."

I mumbled something that I can't remember now. My palms were on the table; she reached out and put her hand over mine and said, "That's nice."

I asked my roommate, Jesse Semple, if he thought I might be able to have an affair with Mrs. Verdery. He told me I was crazy. His exact words were: "Who do you think you are, Dustin Hoffman?" Jesse and I had become firm friends. He was an unusual man. (Dale says all my old friends from school and university are unusual.) He lived in New York City and through his mother, he was on various lists of New York's debutante dances. I got along well with his mother and she got me some invitations, too, which pleased me greatly.

Jesse knew the city well. He knew how to get into jazz clubs and could rattle off the names of every jazz player — famous or obscure — what instrument they played, what record label they were with; everything. His jazz record collection was more important to him than anything else in his life. Jazz could be heard coming out of our room nonstop. To this day, everything I know about jazz, I learned from Jesse, and I still call him for information. He also introduced me to ee cummings and Jack Kerouac. Jesse was his own man — he was very bright and usually saw things from a slightly different perspective than others did. It seemed that every movie we went to together, he had read the book beforehand. I didn't even know that movies could be made from books. In later life, Jesse wrote books on yoga and meditation under the pen name, JJ Semple.

Another classmate, Peter Feller, was selected to be class president. He was not particularly popular, but he had all the qualities of a class president: He strongly supported the school ideals, he was a listener rather than a talker, a good all-around athlete, and a very good student who went on to be a successful Washington, DC lawyer. He got along well with everyone without being particularly close to anyone. He was distant — as if he had something else on his mind. It was difficult to really get to know him. When we met at our 50th class reunion, I revealed that I was writing my memoir. "Everyone has a story," I told him. He said he had an incredible story: His parents had been Russian spies. He hoped to write his story when he retired.

In our last year at school, Jesse, Peter, and I decided that we wanted to go to New York City with three young ladies we'd met at the St. Margaret's School dance. Jesse got us into Birdland, a popular jazz club at the time. The problem was that Peter did not have the funds to go. However, Jesse and I insisted that he join us, so I suggested that since he was the school's president, maybe he could "borrow" the money from the class social fund for which he was responsible. He agreed after some persuasion, and off we went.

After the school holidays, Peter realized that it might be a little difficult to put the money back immediately. He was supported by a scholarship and had a strange relationship with his family. He often spent his holidays at the school rather than at home. In the meantime, Mr. Schwartz, a teacher at the school and our class advisor, found out that Peter had taken the money. I was ashamed that I had come up with the plot, but never had the courage to admit it to Mr. Schwartz. Likewise, I never came to Peter's defense or tried to reduce the level of the seriousness for him by accepting some of the blame myself. We never mentioned the incident again to one another.

At the 50th reunion, I decided to face Peter and remind him of the event. I wanted to tell him how I was never able to forget my behavior and that I was truly sorry. We talked about the incident for nearly an hour. We discussed Mr. Schwartz's reaction, and why Peter agreed to do it. I have to admit I got a little teary-eyed. At the end of our little discussion, I asked him, as a passing remark, how much money was involved.

"Twenty five dollars," he replied. That was a lot of money in those days — worth around $200 now.

In the winter of 1956, my final year, our hockey team was returning from a game against the Gunnery School. I was walking towards the chapel when Mr. Verdery saw me and pulled me aside. He told me that he had talked with a representative of the Boston University Junior College. If I successfully completed my last year at Wooster, I would be accepted at the college the following September. I looked at him in disbelief as if to say, "You mean I'm really going to University?" I just thanked him, but I wanted to do more; give him a hug or something. I couldn't believe it — 14 years of effort, running all the time just to keep up — and I was actually going to attend university.

In April of the year I spent at Loomis, having just returned from a trip to Europe, my father visited me at school. He came back full of enthusiasm for European travel. It was probably the highlight of all his travel experiences. He started a wine collection, got involved in representing a French artist for a New York gallery, and became friends with a very wealthy Englishman who was eventually knighted for his work in television.

After graduation from school, I decided to travel to Europe. I wasn't particularly interested in Europe, but I was interested in doing something different; something quite out of the ordinary. I wanted a new adventure. I remembered back to my reply to my father: "I don't know what I want to do, but it will not be here." Perhaps this was the starting point. Furthermore, I was encouraged to go by my father. I worked for Al Boyson every morning to early afternoon, and in the evenings, I pumped gas at Kovack's gas station. I saved all my money and departed on June 1st, just a week before my sister's wedding.

I flew Icelandic Airways to Prestwick, Scotland, with an eight-hour layover in Reykjavik. The airline hostesses (as they were called in those days) dropped me off at a local hotel bar, the only thing open at two in the morning. It was still daylight. As I was standing at the bar, a young medical student asked if I would like to join him at his table. Sitting with him were two of the most beautiful girls I had ever seen. I could not believe how beautiful and grown up they appeared.

They must have taken a liking to me. "We can call the airline and get them to put you on the next flight," said Divna, who just happened to have won the Miss Iceland title the previous year. "It's in four days' time," she continued. "Meanwhile, we'll show you around Iceland and you can stay with me at my parents' house."

On the last night, we were sitting on the sofa in her mother's house. She let me feel her up. I was so nervous that she had to help me undo her bra. I'd never undone an Icelandic bra before. As I was departing, she reminded me that I had promised to send her a pair of clear plastic, high-heeled shoes that she had seen in an American magazine. What a wonderful introduction to foreign travel.

I landed in Prestwick and took the bus to the center of town. I was planning to ride a BSA Bantam Major motorcycle across Europe and had to pick it up at an address in Prestwick. I showed the address to a policeman and could barely understand a word of what he said. When I finally got to the garage, I had no idea how to drive a motorcycle. All I knew about motorcycles was sitting on a pad on the back of Billy Lovell's Harley Davidson. I received minimum instruction from one of the incomprehensible garage mechanics. It was a miracle that I didn't kill myself or someone else.

My plan was to go north to Fort Williams and see Loch Ness and its monster. Then I would see Edinburgh before riding leisurely down to London. I stayed mostly in B&Bs and had high tea, followed by a beer at the local pub and a huge English breakfast that lasted me until the next high tea. I could never figure out when the English had dinner.

I could not have imagined that travelling throughout Scotland and the north of England in June could be so cold and rainy — it showed how naïve I was. I have no real recollection of any particular sights or experiences except for the lasting memory of the loneliness I felt. People certainly didn't seem as open or friendly as they were in Iceland. I would go to a pub in the evening and have two half pints of bitter (only because I had overheard someone ask for one on my first visit to an English pub). Guinness also seemed popular, but it was more expensive, and I was nervous about running out of money. This was a constant concern throughout the six-week period since I had only saved $500 for the entire trip.

However, all that changed when I arrived in London. I stayed with my father's friend, Dick Meyer, and enjoyed the life of the rich. He had a huge apartment in Albert Hall Mansions, which had two types of toilet paper in every bathroom: the waxed English kind and "an American imported type for my wife and guests." The Myers had a beautiful daughter, Sofia.

She was outgoing, friendly, and introduced me to her public school friends. She was only two years older, but seemed much more mature and worldly than any girl I had previously met. I concluded at the end of my six weeks that all young Europeans seemed better educated, more cultured, and more mature than students in America. I think Sofia enjoyed riding on the back of my motorcycle, and she encouraged me to stay longer in London. I had a wonderful time being taken around London by her and joining her social life. Having extended it from five days to two weeks, I suppose my stay in London was the highlight of my trip. The remaining three weeks were speeding through France (with a required visit to Pigalle) and on to Italy, going from one museum's front steps to the next, sharing experiences with other young adventurers.

Thirty-three years later, we bought a ground floor apartment in Courtfield Gardens, South Kensington; not far from the Albert Hall Mansions where the Meyers and their beautiful daughter lived. I often pass the mansions as I retrace my footsteps to the bus stop, remembering how I was instructed to raise my hand in order to stop the world-renowned double-decker bus. I never imagined that one day I would actually live in this city and take a similar bus to work every day.

I think about this often. Whenever we go by Albert Hall or pass the Prince Albert Memorial, I think about how far I have come in my life. I would never have imagined that my life would be so eventful or that my trip to England would prove to be the start of a lifelong adventure. I think about how far I've come from Newtown, Connecticut, Al Boyson, and Uncle Herbert, which is one reason why I'm writing this book.

After a six-week period, it was time to return to America. I motorcycled to the French port of Le Havre to locate the ship to New York the following morning. It was an American liner and I asked the steward if I could put my motorcycle on board and pick it up on the pier in New York. He allowed me to do so and stated that when they arrived at Pier 3, my motorcycle would be unloaded and left on the dockside. In the meantime, I flew to New York, went to Pier 3 and, quite incredibly, there my motorcycle was, resting against a post just as the man in Le Harve said it would be. I drove along the Merritt Parkway to my home in Newtown, arriving completely unexpected and unannounced. I walked into the kitchen after being away for six weeks and said hello.

"David, you're so thin!" my mother exclaimed.

My money had lasted; I even had some left over. From that first travel experience, I would continue to travel for the rest of my life. I have either visited or worked in 38 countries to date and am off to Sri Lanka in four months' time.

College

Boston University had established a junior college to take almost any student with a high school degree or equivalent (including a "certificate of experience" for Korean War vets). If successful at the end of the two years, students received an Associate of Arts degree. If they achieved a B average grade, they could transfer to the university to work towards a full college, Bachelor of Arts degree. The junior college was something of a last chance for everyone who attended.

Boston University Junior College

Twenty-seven years later, my son, Adam, followed the same path. Not for the reasons that held me back — to the contrary. He was very bright, fluent in French, Italian, and Arabic, and an avid reader. He didn't apply himself. For prep school, he was accepted to Phillips Exeter Academy, but decided to remain at St. Stephen's School in Rome. He said Italian girls were prettier and more interesting than those in Exeter, New Hampshire. Since he didn't bother to study, Boston University Junior College became his last chance, too.

At the first day of college orientation, the head of the college spoke to our class of 300 people. At one point during his talk, he asked us to look at the student to our left then look at the student to our right: "One of these two students will not be here for the second year of college. For most of you, this will be your last opportunity to further your education," he said. I knew there would be no more chances for me. I was unprepared for the real world. The thought of being a milkman for the rest of my life, like Al Boyson, was more than I could bear. Of course, another option was joining the Army, something many friends in my situation had done. But because I had a history of osteomyelitis, I was considered unfit for military services, so I could neither be drafted nor could I join. I had to succeed at Boston University Junior College.

The college was located near the Boston Public Library, while the main campus was about three miles north, on Commonwealth Avenue. There wasn't much of a university atmosphere during my first two years there; in fact, I lived in a converted hotel, built in 1925. Miles Standish Hall became a college dormitory in 1948. Because it was located near Fenway Park, Babe Ruth used to occupy Room 818 whenever the Yankees played the Red Sox at Fenway. My room was on the floor below.

Still enthralled by the six weeks I had spent motorcycling through Europe that summer, I arrived at Boston University with a beard, wearing a boat-necked striped shirt, tight black trousers, and a Marlon Brando haircut. I liked to think I looked Parisian, but I couldn't fool a Frenchman. At the university, I was immediately classified by my four roommates as bohemian and as such, an intellectual.

The living quarters consisted of suites divided into rooms for five students. Each of the living quarters had three bedrooms, a suite, and a living area. I weighed 145 pounds (65 kg) and was 5'8" (1.72m) tall (if I stood up straight). My four roommates were varsity football players on athletic scholarships. They agreed that they had never met someone quite like me before. They immediately nicknamed me Plato and assumed I was very intelligent, very rich, and a bit of a sissy.

I, on the other hand, was overwhelmed by their lifestyle. Charles "Chick" Wynowski came from Norwalk, Connecticut, a lower-middle-class town. His aim was to be a salesman for a whisky company — this despite the fact that he did not drink or smoke. Dave McDermott was from Lowell, Massachusetts, a rusty manufacturing city. I forget the names of the third and fourth players, but I do remember that one of them had no neck and part of his daily routine was to climb the 12 flights of the fire escape while carrying a rucksack full of weights. I had to climb over a couple of barbells and a huge punching bag to reach my room. Except for Chick, the future whisky salesman, all the others attended the College of Physical Education and would all eventually become PE instructors.

Living with them suited me. I rather liked the idea of being around such different (for me) people from unfamiliar backgrounds. I was intrigued by their regimented, conservative lifestyles. They were just as curious about me. They were all very neat and tidy, even fastidious, like my mother. They were clean-shaven and got a haircut every two weeks. They spent hours polishing their shoes and were careful about what they ate. They woke at the same time every day, except on Sundays when they had an extra hour of sleep before going to the gym to review mistakes made in the game the previous day. Even after the game each Saturday, they rarely complained of a sore foot or bruised rib or swollen wrist. Nothing short of a leg in a plaster cast — which happened to one of them — ever drew complaints. I used to ask, "But doesn't it hurt when you get tackled or kicked? Aren't you ever afraid?"

"Not really." They said it as though the thought never entered their minds. I never understood why they weren't afraid. I was terrified whenever I played American football. It was the price you paid for acceptance in a private boarding school. In University I only played intramural college hockey.

I studied hard for my B average, got my Associate of Arts degree, and transferred to the College of Liberal Arts. I promptly failed two courses and was put on academic probation. As a matter of policy, the university sent letters out to the party responsible for the student's fees, advising them of his status (no longer true today). I remember the incident well. I was home when the letter arrived. My father came into the kitchen from his office and said, in an almost offhand way, "I got a letter from the university." I knew exactly what it said.

"I guess you know what you have to do," he added, and that was that. He didn't get mad and he didn't ask why. He didn't even seem disappointed. I wasn't sure if he was simply treating me like an adult or if he had reached the end of his tether after 16 years of trying to educate me.

Boston University College of Liberal Arts

At the College of Liberal Arts, I began a BA degree in psychology. I admit this was one of the easier routes to a bachelor's degree. I knew I wasn't going to become a psychologist, but my first priority was simply to get a college degree, to be able to say I had been to university. I had no further goal or career objective.

At the end of my first year, I decided not to continue living in a college dormitory and joined a college fraternity, Lambda Chi Alpha. To my surprise, I enjoyed living in the fraternity. A group of 25 young men from vaguely similar backgrounds sharing social aspects of a university life — it had a slightly preppy atmosphere, but not to the degree that I had experienced in boarding school. After my European experience, I rather preferred the bohemian lifestyle. I indulged myself, but I couldn't embrace it totally. My roots were too deeply set in the middle class with its basic family values. I was a bohemian with a small "b"; perhaps I was simply unconventional, rather than bohemian. My fraternity considered me a nonconformist, an artistic type, though I could not draw, paint, or play the guitar. I was identified with the beat generation of Jack Kerouac, but I always got to my 8:00 AM class on time. I really didn't know who or what I was.

Freddy Bazler — a neighbor, part-time student at the university, and a folk music enthusiast — rented a warehouse near the apartment I shared with my roommate, Ben. As we passed the warehouse on our way to university one day, we stopped to look in just to see what was happening. In the way of a greeting, Freddy immediately shouted at us to come in. He spoke enthusiastically about how he was going to turn the warehouse into a coffee house and call it the Golden Vanity, the name of a ship in some folk song.

It was one of Boston's very early coffee houses, places where young people came to drink only coffee, tea, or Coca Cola. There was no alcohol or drugs (the dope would come a few years later), and it was designed around folk singing. It was a venue for people interested in folk music or people who wanted to play and sing folk songs. Woody Guthrie and Pete Seeger made guest appearances. Talented students would perform there, including a first-year art student named Joan Baez.

Whenever we passed the warehouse, Freddy would ask if we could "just give me a hand moving these barrels from the truck"; or "give me a hand putting table tops on the barrels"; and then give him a hand with this or that so that Ben and I ended up being the official dishwashers and substitute waiters, but our tips were not nearly as good as those received by the waitresses.

We spent nearly as much time at the Golden Vanity as we did in our apartment. It became part of our social life. Joan would sing on the fire escape of the College of Performing Arts during lunch break. Everybody passing by would stop to listen. She was a relaxed and friendly person, oblivious to what was ahead of her (or maybe she wasn't).

Another good friend was Sam Notorantonio. He was a first-generation Italian from Providence, Rhode Island. We became good friends and planned a six-week trip to Mexico one summer. He was extremely bright, majoring in some sort of complex physics I could never understand. He was very unhappy with university life and wanted to break away from family tradition and the pressure put on him by his immigrant parents. His father owned two Ford dealerships in Providence and was financially successful, with a certain status in the Italian community.

Sam would go home every weekend to see his girlfriend of three years. They had been together since high school. According to Sam, her father was fairly high up in Rhode Island's Italian Mafia. While at university, his first time away from home, Sam fell in love with a Jewish girl from Long Island. She was lovely with a beautiful figure, curious, intelligent, and a wonderfully deep laugh. Sam was afraid to end the relationship with his school sweetheart because of the possible retaliation from her Mafioso parents.

Mexico 1958

In the summer of 1958, just before our last year at college, Sam Notorantonio and I decided to play Jack Kerouac and go "On the Road." But we did it in style. Sam had a new 1957 Ford convertible. We calculated the cost and in mid-July, got into his car with two other friends, Chris Kazan (the son of Elia Kazan, the famous movie and theatre director) and Bruno, a friend of Chris's. They were both students at Harvard University. The four of us drove nonstop to Mexico City where we rented a two-bedroom apartment and spent our first two weeks getting to know the city. Four young men and a fancy new convertible made for blurred memories. We did what we thought was expected of the "beat generation": spent the day drinking beer and indulged in the occasional marijuana cigarette. That was my only drug experience. But marijuana seemed to be almost normal in Mexico. Pulque was the cheapest form of alcohol at the time. It cost only pennies for a gallon and was made from the juice of cactus. It looked like lime-colored sperm. The peasants would dip their fingers in it and give it to their babies to suck on to stop them from crying. It put the babies in a daylong stupor (not unlike us), particularly if their stomachs were empty. It was foul tasting stuff, nearly as bad as the penicillin I used to take.

We drifted. We went to bullfights, went to whorehouses, roamed the streets. We just seemed to be wandering around the city, soaking up the foreignness and poverty. We were big on just hanging out. I have no recollection of any sightseeing except for the Aztec Ruins.

After Mexico City, we travelled south to Oaxaca. We spent our evenings in different small-town squares, sitting around and watching young girls strolling one way and the men strolling in the opposite direction. On our Mexico trip, we usually stayed at one place for two nights and then moved on to the next small town. Sitting in a town square next to a new Ford convertible with the top down would attract young lads of the town (the girls were too shy). Chris, Sam, and Bruno all spoke some Spanish, and they asked the boys if they would like a ride in the car. It was always a hassle among the young lads as to which two would sit in the front seat. Off they would go, guiding Sam along the streets where they knew they were most likely to see their friends, followed by a couple of turns around the town square for good measure. That was the way we got information about the local social life, which was usually a bar or a whorehouse.

The young Mexican village girls looked very seductive with their olive skin, dark eyes, and full breasts, but we found that you could not do anything unless you agreed to marry one first. In one small town, just south of Oaxaca, was a whorehouse with a single row of hammocks (with curtains for "privacy"). One lady at the end of the row had hydrocephalus, which meant she had water on the brain. We decided at this point that it was time to head home.

We got into the car after watching the local bullfight and for the next four days drove nonstop, with a bushel of peaches and just enough money for gas. As soon as I got home, I started scratching around my crotch area, which seemed to be on fire. I couldn't stop scratching. When I could no longer bear it, I told my father. He suggested we go into his office where I learned that I had a severe case of crabs. My father had to shave the local area and then sent me to the local pharmacist for a lotion, asking as I left, "Been sleeping in cheap hotels or with cheap women?" Thankfully, he gave me the option of saying which of the two I'd actually done.

Naturally, my mother wanted to know what was wrong, and as any mother would, she overreacted. My father and I were more amused than concerned. You can imagine my mother, whose pleasure in life was ironing, vacuuming, and just generally cleaning the house. The horror she felt on finding that her son was infecting her house with crabs was to be expected: She immediately stripped all the beds (remember, we're a family of seven) — including mattress covers — and washed all the sheets and bedspreads. The smell of disinfectant in our house lasted for days. Since it was the end of August, we started having all our meals on the back veranda. My parents were friends with Chris's parents, who soon discovered that he had the same problem. My mother could not wait for university to start again.

Senior Year

The fourth and final year at Boston University would be the longest and most anxiety-producing year of my life. I did not have a relationship with anybody. I spent my time alone studying in the library, but I knew I wouldn't be able to graduate.

In my third year, I met Sandra Rosenquist. She was a lovely girl who came from a background similar to mine. She had blonde hair, tied behind her head, and an angular face with a fresh Nordic look. She was a serious student, majoring in philosophy, the type that you take home to meet the family. Our relationship lasted about a year and a half. I thought I was in love. In fact, I was in love. The problem was she was "wife material," but I wasn't up to being hers, or anybody else's, husband.

By the end of my fourth year at university in 1960, I hadn't completed the necessary credits to graduate. I knew my father would stick to our agreement, that he would pay my university fees and provide a modest living allowance for a four-year period only. After that, I was on my own.

I was 24 and Sandra was 23. During the summer, she got a job in her hometown of Providence, Rhode Island, and I worked at the Dry Dock Savings Bank on Lexington Avenue and 56th Street (which is now defunct). We spent weekends together, either in my tiny single room on 25th Street and Third Avenue in New York City or in one of our hometowns. Sandra was mentally prepared for marriage; I wasn't "fully formed" enough to even consider it.

I was scared about being out in the world on my own for the first time, with no degree and without any qualifications for a decent job, and a wife to support. I knew then that the relationship was doomed. I couldn't talk about the future because at that point there wasn't one. I phoned her from New York while she was in Providence and told her that I couldn't continue the relationship. When she asked why, all I could do was repeat that I couldn't continue the relationship.

I started to get stomachaches and couldn't eat. Eventually, I became sick and had to go the infirmary. The doctor recommended a diet of consommé soup and toast. That was all I ate for two months. Taking Benzedrine or Dexedrine to stay awake for the final exams may have partly caused my loss of appetite. I went to see my favorite teacher, Professor Carr. He was officially retired, but he continued to teach the classes he liked.

Three or four of us would meet him before or after class at a diner across the street from the college. If we asked him about a current event, his ready response was, "I'm only up to the early 18th century in my reading." Whenever he explained a theory, concept, a military battle, or the dynamics of a relationship — whatever the subject — he would illustrate his points with salt and peppershakers, a paper napkin dispenser, a ketchup bottle, and a sugar container. These would be moved around as he talked through the subject. In contrast to the other teachers, he seemed to derive joy simply out of seeing the students 's responses.

I went to him to discuss my dilemma. "By June first, I will be on my own," I said to him. "Four years at Boston University without a degree is sort of a waste of time, isn't it?" He assured me that I was no different from many other students, and it was often a natural order of events.

He told me it was simple. "You are being thrown out of the nest," he said. "You don't think you are ready and your father thinks that you should be. He has made his point." He took the salt and pepper shakers and moved them around. My biggest academic problem was satisfying a language requirement, he thought. The other courses, he said, could be dealt with easily. The napkin holder came crashing down on the table. He had a plan.

Professor Carr suggested I enter a Spanish language-training program at a university in Mexico City for a three-month period. It required three hours of instruction per day plus supervised study. I could then transfer the results back to Boston to satisfy my language requirements.

"Now you've got one thing sorted out," he moved the napkin dispenser to one side. Then he suggested I go to the University of California, Los Angeles (UCLA), where I could qualify to take courses as a California resident for only seven dollars a term if I lived there for six months. "Do your remaining two courses there. Transfer those grades back to Boston University. You'll receive your degree in the mail in 1961 instead of 1960." Professor Carr and his salt and peppershakers, along with a napkin dispenser, a bottle of ketchup, and a sugar container helped a spoiled, self-pitying, immature young man go out into the world.

I recently found a letter that my father had written to my sister Elaine, two years after my meeting with Professor Carr. It read:

"Well, your brother has finally come back home. He went to Mexico and lived in California, and got his university degree. He got married, got his first good job with the Red Cross in the states of Washington and Alaska, got divorced, and here he is, back home — all in the space of two years."

What he didn't tell me was that he called the FBI to see if they knew anything of my whereabouts.

The Carr Plan

While waiting for a bus at the end of the first day of registration at the University of Mexico, I met a young lady, Jeanette, with long, tied up, dark hair. She was slightly taller than I was and very smartly dressed for the first day of school. I felt rather scruffy standing beside her. She was from Beverly Hills, California, in her last year of studying Russian at Stanford University. She had decided to take a course in Spanish "just for fun." She liked to travel and so decided to come to the university.

"I like languages," she said. She was bright, focused, and we were both interested in travel and came from similar backgrounds. I asked her out on a few dates. She never turned me down. We spent our free time together throughout the program. This did nothing to help me to learn Spanish. But, then again, knowing my difficulty with language, I wouldn't have been any better off had I kept company with a young olive-skinned Mexican beauty.

On reflection, it seems my days were completely taken up with classes, studying in the evenings and seeing Jeanette whenever possible. I got through my classes only because I established a relationship with my Spanish teacher early in the program. He had a vague connection to a farm that raised fighting bulls. He showed me pictures of himself training to be a bullfighter. I asked if anyone could take lessons. "Of course," he said, and for the rest of the program we talked (only talked) about me training to be a matador. He was convinced that I would do well. He said that I could live with his family and practice every day. We developed a good relationship throughout the three months of lessons, thus ensuring that I would get a passing grade and satisfy my language requirement according to the Carr Plan. In the meantime, Jeanette sailed through her course. I couldn't believe how easy she made it seem.

While I was there, I met a student walking through the main reception area at the university, a guy I had seen before at Boston University and always been a little curious about, but had never spoken with. As soon as we saw one another, we immediately shook hands and talked excitedly about how we had to come 4,000 miles to say hello. We were both bohemians, except that Sunny was an authentic Bohemian with a capital "B." I was just looking for a new identity. For a black person, he was fair skinned, with striking good looks, and a small gold earring in his left ear. This was 1960 — and that was quite uncommon at the time. He was slim, fit, and always wore flip-flops. He smoked marijuana "only on the weekends" and lived with his wife, Laura, in a "pad" on the Santa Monica beachfront. "If you're ever in California, stop by. We always have an extra bed," he offered.

I never realized this casual, off the hand remark or invitation would turn out to be an extremely important part of the Carr Plan. Two months after this fortuitous meeting, after completing my Spanish requirement, I would be on my way to UCLA to sign up for the remaining credits I needed to obtain my degree. Sunny and his wife would provide me with accommodations and the only friendships I established while working during the day and going to college in the evening.

At the end of the Spanish program, I decided to spend some time travelling in the Yucatán before starting phase two of the Carr Plan, I asked Jeanette if she would join me. "I would love to," she said. We took a train from Mexico City to the Yucatán, staying in Mérida and Chichinitza, in simple shelters near the beach. The train ride was pretty rough. The train went at 15 miles an hour and had only wooden benches for seats. There were whole families on it, with chickens, small pigs, and goats getting on and off the train throughout the night. We had never experienced anything so primitive.

During our travels, we began to fall in love. It wasn't a bolt-out-of-the-sky type of falling in love. We just sort of slipped into it. Backpacking in a foreign country and looking for support from only each other, an emotional dependency developed. At the end of our trip, we went to California — she to her family in Beverly Hills and then on to finish her college education at Stanford, and in accordance with the Carr Plan, I to Los Angeles to enroll in UCLA to register for my remaining two courses. While doing so, I remembered that my bohemian friend, Sunny, had extended an invitation to me when we were in Mexico: *If you're ever in California, stop by. We always have an extra bed.*

Sunny and Laura, who was white, well-educated, and from a wealthy Colorado banking family, welcomed me with open arms. Neither of them was working and they were living in a very comfortable four-bedded house, not more than fifty feet from the sands of the Santa Monica beach. I assumed Sunny was living off Laura's allowance. When I first described Sunny, after meeting him in Mexico, I said he was a Bohemian with a capital "B". Well, if it wasn't classical Bohemian, it was certainly an indescribable lifestyle — maybe it was Hollywood Bohemian.

Their home was like a boarding house for "far out" Hollywood hopefuls. A steady stream of black and white post-college students or permanent college students, or just "hangers on" would come and go. None of them seemed to have jobs. But all were "just about to get one" in some business on the fringes in the movie world. One guest was a "model," built in the style of Marilyn Monroe and who had quite a few boyfriends — both black and white. Another was a chauffeur for a Hollywood movie director —a job that lasted until the director realized he didn't know Los Angeles. Another was a trumpet player, always looking for a "gig." The records (yes, vinyl records) of Charlie Parker, Chet Baker, John Coltrane, Sonny Rollins, Ray Charles, and Thelonious Monk were played from morning to night. There was a permanent smell of marijuana in the air, but I was never aware of hard drugs. And there was a large amount of casual sex. Once, in the hallway, Sunny and Laura were fornicating in the open. The following day, I asked Laura if she wasn't a little embarrassed. Her reply: "Hell, no. I was just glad he was fucking me instead of some other chick — as he usually does."

"Why didn't you use your own bed?" I asked.

"Someone else got there first."

Sunny had one problem — a chip on his shoulder. Once while we were driving along Wilshire Boulevard in his Austin Healy 100 sports car, a policeman stopped him. He asked the usual questions, including "Where do you work?" Sunny replied: "I don't." The next obvious question: "What do you do?" "Nothing" was Sunny's reply. Naturally, an altercation ensued and Sunny, being extremely articulate, put down the officer with every question. Sunny's final comment to me was: "If I was white like you, I wouldn't get hassled."

Out of the clear blue one day, Laura said, "David, I was talking to a guy who works for the International Red Cross (IRC) and he was telling me that they send people all over the world."

Boston University accepted my credits from the University of Mexico and UCLA and mailed my diploma to me in California. And, I was able to accept the position as Assistant Field Director in the IRC and immediately started my training in Tacoma, Washington.

First Steps

Jeanette and I married the same month, in Sacramento, California, in a lovely garden at her grandparents' residence. The only clear memory I have of our wedding is a long row of eucalyptus trees on either side of a long drive leading to a Spanish-style hacienda with lovely gardens.

Jeanette

My first work assignment was at Fort Lewis in Tacoma, Washington, about twenty miles from Seattle, where I received my training to be an Assistant Field Director. We lived there for about eight months before I was given my first overseas assignment.

Fort Lewis was a huge Army post with a main Red Cross office plus two sub-offices. There were seven of us. We had all just graduated from university and this was our first job. I enjoyed the training experience. My job was to be a counselor to the young Army recruits who were experiencing domestic issues that might in some way affect their military efficiency. What made the counseling interesting was dealing with a vast array of personal and domestic problems that the young recruits, as well as their wives and family, had.

Essentially, we would receive a telex from a local Red Cross Chapter in any one of the 50 states, saying that some parent knew only that their son had joined the army, but had no idea where he had been assigned or what condition he might be in. Our job was to contact the man, interview him, and send a report back to the local chapter. Generally, the solider was fine, but too lazy to write his family. Occasionally, he would be in the stockade or had gone AWOL.

Other times, a soldier's wife would be having difficulty adjusting to her new environment or to the relationship. A soldier once told me that his German wife went with their daughter to East Germany to visit her family and now the authorities were refusing her permission to leave. That was one of the very few cases where families were reunited through official government channels.

The work suited me very well. I like people and I liked solving their problems. Our offices were open from 8:00 AM to 5:00 PM every day. On Sundays, we took turns manning the main office in case of emergency. If it was after hours, someone was on call. I went one Sunday to relieve the weekend duty officer. All the lights were off. The front door was locked. When I unlocked it, I found him sitting under a single light reading a book. I said, "People will think we're not open." He replied, "A sign says to call an emergency number." I protested that there were no phones around. "That's their problem," he said. He was not a happy man; I don't think he liked his work.

Jeanette and I enjoyed living in Tacoma. We lived modestly, but were able to do as we wanted. I bought a 1956 MG sports car. It was a wonderful area to tour and all new to Jeanette and me, so we spent our spare time exploring the northwest.

Jeanette got a job at the local welfare office in Tacoma. She didn't find it too interesting, but it filled her time while we waited for my first overseas assignment. We were led to believe we would go to Japan; hence, we took Japanese lessons together at the local college. Our life as newlyweds was as I expected. We respected one another and had common values. We were able to compromise when necessary and we talked about what went on between us. But Jeanette was more taciturn than I was. I was accustomed to wearing my heart on my sleeve. We agreed that we did not want any children. We enjoyed being with each other.

In the evenings, we read, listened to music — she introduced me to classical music — and we played chess. We did not have a television. I would talk to her about my work and she would read over my correspondence to reassure me that the letters were grammatically correct and written intelligently. I was conscious of my handicap.

On the other hand, our romance lacked passion. We made love almost every night, but we were both aware that our sex life was not as we felt it should be. The relationship lacked energy and a certain excitement. My father's words came back to me: "Do not underestimate the value of a good sex life." In today's current value system, we would have simply lived together and then parted. But in those days, you had to get married to live with somebody.

Upon receiving notice of my first overseas assignment, we were a little disappointed to learn that we would spend two years in Anchorage, Alaska, before going to Japan. For some reason, the Red Cross thought of Alaska as overseas. The head of the office, Mr. Calkins, was an excellent instructor and a very good first boss. He was a retired naval officer, experienced in training, supervising, and advising young men. He knew we were disappointed not to go to Japan. "David, you don't have to go to Alaska," he said. "But if you want a better assignment next time and you want to get along in an organization, it is always advisable to accept your first assignment."

Driving up the Alaskan Highway together was to be our second great adventure after Mexico. We felt like pioneers. Instead of a covered wagon, we bought a new Volkswagen. The road was dirt in 1961 and due to the extreme climate, it had to be constantly maintained by huge yellow road scrapers. We passed through small settlements, each one called something like "Milestone 15" or "Milestone 28." They generally had a diner, a garage with two gas pumps in front, a motel, a few A-frame houses, some house trailers, and sometimes a prefabricated schoolhouse, often with broken-down cars, pick-up trucks, and farm equipment scattered about. We drove for miles without seeing another car and occasionally, the biggest trucks in the world would pass us going south. They were loaded with Jurassic-sized tree trunks. The ruggedness was a little intimidating — majestic vistas, huge rock outgrowths, lakes, rivers, and pine forests.

Three days after we started, we arrived at Fort Richardson to begin our assignment. The work routine was the same as in Washington, except we were a small operation — two men and a woman.

Jeanette soon found a job working at the federal land-grant office. Interesting people applied for free land. They would be given 25 acres on which they were required to farm for a specified period of time, after which the land was transferred to the homesteader's ownership. Settlers could apply for a loan to build a house and purchase the required equipment. Jeanette didn't particularly enjoy her work, but it suited her for the time being.

Our relationship continued but without spirit, without any real life-long commitment to one another. We drifted along. I knew something was wrong, but neither of us was willing to look deeper to make a real connection.

Shortly before Christmas in 1962, I was at my office, waiting for Jeanette to pick me up, when a colleague called from her office to explain that Jeanette had to take a client to a site. She might be late and the woman on the phone would pick me up instead. When I was dropped off at our house, I noticed that our car was already in the drive. She must have gotten home earlier than expected.

"Hi, I'm home," I called out. No answer. *She must be in the bathroom*, I thought. I opened the cloakroom door to hang up my coat and noticed her coat and hat were not there. *That's odd*, I thought. I went to the bedroom and opened the closet. It was empty.

She had carefully removed only those items that clearly belonged to her or things given to us by her family and friends. I got the same feeling in my chest as when I'd be suddenly frightened, the way it feels when you sense danger. I sat down.

The phone rang. "David, I know you are worried but I am safe," she said. "I have left you. I'm with William" (a work colleague assigned to Elmendorf, the Air Force base on the other side of Anchorage).

"Are you going to stay with him? Do you love him?"

"No, he is just the catalyst. I couldn't do it on my own."

Then she hung up. I never saw or heard from her again.

It was planned and executed in such a surgical manner. Later that night, Ann, William's wife called. "I guess you know that your wife is with my husband. He did the same thing when we were in Germany. I'm not worried. It's happened a lot. He'll be back."

I cry easily. In movies, watching TV, seeing a marching band pass by, hearing taps at night, and seeing a friend walking back down the aisle after saying "I do." But this time I didn't cry. I sat in the large comfortable chair in the living room and stared at the floor. I must have sat there for an hour. I didn't throw a plate, slam the door, or call a friend. I just sat there. It was like somebody had just died.

I simply didn't anticipate it. She did it without warning because I would have tried to change her mind and she didn't want it changed. I hadn't seen the depth of her unhappiness, her disappointment, her desperation.

I remembered that she got home late once. I asked her where she had been. "It's almost Christmas so you shouldn't ask too many questions," she said. I naively thought she was getting me something for my birthday, which is the day after Christmas. Perhaps I just didn't want to see it. I did what I had learned to do in such circumstances: nothing. I was not going to call the police. I was not going to go out and search the city. Instead, I repeatedly went over the events of our relationship in my mind.

I got on with my job and became very close to a young married officer and his family. They were great outdoorsy people and very happy to be living in Alaska. That was very good for me because there was only one other option — to spend my time with others who hated the country and were waiting to return to the southern 48. I went camping, skiing, hunting, and salmon fishing with them and their friends. I also acted as a volunteer babysitter so they could go out.

Through my work, I occasionally had reason to visit or obtain information from local hospitals. The role of the hospital administrator rather appealed to me. It seemed like it would be a satisfying career and might be something I could do, but I gave it no further thought at the time. However, when Jeanette left, I was able to reevaluate my life. The divorce law required that I live in Alaska for a year before being eligible to apply for a divorce. I decided that after that one year, I would return to Connecticut and attempt to gain admission into one of dozens of graduate training programs in public health and hospital administration.

As it was an uncontested divorce, the procedure was simple. I did not have to go to court; I simply signed some papers, and that was that. Today, I have no idea where the document is, and I have never been asked to provide any information or confirmation about it.

Columbia

If I had to put a date on when I grew up, it would be in 1963, at age 27. I had some modest savings and two years of work experience. Responsible only for myself, I resigned from the Red Cross, packed a single suitcase, and departed from Anchorage, returning to my hometown in Connecticut. It would be a new start to my life. I was going to be a hospital administrator. It seemed to me like a good job, working with people, purposeful, respectable, and community-spirited. It suited me and my "do-gooder" attitude.

I arranged to meet with Dr. Clay, who was the director of the department for hospital administration in the School of Public Health at Columbia University in New York City. Dr. Clay, like Professor Carr at Boston University, outlined for me exactly what I would need to do in order to gain acceptance in the program:

1) Go to Columbia University's special undergraduate studies program and take three courses: economics, business administration, and accounting.
2) Obtain at least a B in each of the above courses.
3) While doing the above, accept a job in the admitting office of the Brooklyn Medical Center in order to have some hospital experience.

If I fulfilled these three conditions, he would accept me into the two-year program starting in September 1964. I was pleased with the way the interview went.

At the same time, the Reverend John D. Verdery, the headmaster at Wooster School, provided me with an excellent recommendation. He recounted the story in his memoir, Partial Recall:

"Then there is David, to whom I shall give no last name because he is still very much alive and well. Academically, David was one of the worst students I have ever known. During all his secondary-school years (which were spent at several schools and many summer schools), I don't think he ever actually passed anything. But he was just about as nice a young human as I have ever known. Each year, at the final faculty meeting, his fate would be debated. Each year, it would be agreed that he had absolutely no academic future and that he really should be let go. Then someone would say, 'But how can we possibly let such a nice guy go? We need him. Guys like that don't come along every day. If we can't find a way to hang on to David, and do a little something for him, then there is something wrong with us.'

So, we would find a way and he would stay; until one fine day he actually received a diploma. I have no idea how many credits he had, and I can't even remember where he went to college. He came to see me a few years later, looking for a little career advice. He seemed stumped because his education did not seem to fit him into any of the neat molds of our society. On the spur of the moment, I said, 'David, why don't you just go out and do some good? Get a job with the Red Cross or something. They don't have people like you walking through their doors looking for work every day.'

So he got a job with the Red Cross, spent several years in faraway places, doing a lot of good and a lot of thinking.

Then he came back and said, 'I've decided that I want to be a hospital administrator and I've applied to Colombia. Will you write me a recommendation?' I thought of his Wooster transcript and my heart sank. With all those asterisks, indicating where this course or that course had been made up, and with what grade, it looked as though a hen with dirty feet had walked across it. And now he wanted to go to Columbia? But I said of course I would. I ended up writing something that was entirely true, entirely supportive, and that was all that needed to be said; and Columbia, to its great credit, read it right and accepted him. I wrote: 'This young man can do anything he says he will do.'"[3]

My sister agreed that I could live with her and her husband in Greenwich Village until I found a place of my own. This turned out to be a single room with use of an adjoining bathroom in a large apartment occupied by an elderly Jewish couple. I learned at the end of my first week just how Orthodox they were. I came back to my room late one Friday night and noticed that they had left the burner on in the kitchen. I turned it off and went to bed. The following morning I heard a knock on my door and a plaintive voice.

"Please, Mr. Egee, would you kindly turn the burner back on so we can have our breakfast?"

---

3   *Partial Recall: The Afterthoughts of a Schoolmaster* - John D. Verdery. Atheneum Books, 1981, pp. 35-36.

At the time, it was news to me that Orthodox Jews do not use a car, entertain friends, or leave the house on Saturdays. They cannot make a fire or use the telephone. The husband was always bent over a desk in a darkened room, reading a book with something that looked like a scarf hanging from his neck. The entire apartment was hidden from the day by heavy curtains. In the corner, a single desk lamp illuminated his book.

The lifestyle suited me. The atmosphere was conducive to only one thing: studying. For the entire year, I went from the front door directly to my room. It felt like they were hiding from something. Could it be me? We hardly spoke except for greetings. Their daughter once visited. "How do you like living in a mausoleum?" she asked me.

I enjoyed my night job even though it was a grueling experience. I worked from midnight to 8:00 AM and then went to my room and slept for six hours. I had three hour-long classes, three days a week. The rest of the time was for studying, usually in the library. The remainder of the day was filled with classes, study, and naps. Travelling back to the city after working all night, I once collapsed onto the floor of the train — I had fallen asleep while standing.

Towards the end of my accounting course, the teacher took me aside after class. He asked me why I was taking the introductory course to accounting and whether I planned to go any further in the subject. I explained that my acceptance to the graduate program of public health was conditional on taking this particular course, achieving a B average.

"So you do not intend to take any more courses in accountancy?"

"No sir, I do not."

"I think that is a good idea. We might be able to manage a B," he smiled knowingly.

The first year of graduate school was mostly practical demonstrations, reading assignments, and written reports, all to do with the management of a hospital. It wasn't difficult work, but there was a lot of it. I think they were testing our endurance. We were a class of 15; only two dropped out. If succeeding in hospital administration simply involved long hours and hard work, I had finally hit my stride. I couldn't win on any academic tests, but I would come first on any endurance tests.

Succeeding in your first year was the hardest. The second was a mix of practical and academic assignments. It included a four-month management internship at a hospital. Most of my classmates wanted to be assigned to big city hospitals, and the married students wanted hospitals close to their families. The two nuns in our class wanted to be assigned to a Catholic hospital. I took a fancy to one of them and we sometimes had lunch together, but it never went anywhere. We were always chaperoned by her colleague nun.

I asked Dr. Clay if there were any Columbia-approved teaching hospitals in a rural area. He said there was a "very exciting" hospital in Flemington, New Jersey, doing some interesting work integrating the local GPs into the hospital's educational programs. All of the specialists in the area have their offices in the hospital itself. They received referrals only from the GPs practicing throughout the county. My classmates wondered why I wanted to go to the sticks when I could be in New York City, Boston, or Pittsburgh. One asked if I was planning on going into veterinarian hospital administration.

I think what attracted me back to a rural community was that I had wonderful memories of the small town in which I grew up and of all the schools I went to that were situated in small communities. After university life in Boston and New York City, perhaps I wanted to repeat my life in an environment I enjoyed so much.

I took up my internship at the Huntingdon Medical Center, in rural Flemington, New Jersey. The 60-bed hospital with an extensive outpatient department served the entire county. My internship was, in effect, to act as a gofer for Mr. Grant, the hospital administrator. I took the minutes of meetings he attended, sat in on other hospital meetings, and wrote up reports on management issues within the hospital. I learned how to make perfect gin and tonics and scotch and sodas ("Three cubes, David."). To start with, I didn't know the ice had to go in first and that the small lemons ("Always small ones, David.") had to be cut in quarters. I, not Mr. Grant, served them at each board of trustees meeting.

I soon learned that while Mr. Grant had the official title of hospital administrator, the real power lay with the medical director, Dr. Henderson. He reported directly to the chairman of the board of trustees, not Mr. Grant, the hospital administrator.

Among the hospital's extensive expansion program was an intensive care unit, which was then a new way of managing patients after complicated surgery. Dr. Henderson called me to his office. I met him only at meetings or passing in the corridors, but that was it. "How would you like to give the chief of medicine a hand in establishing the equipment needs for the new intensive care unit?" he asked. I was delighted. It would give me a chance to work with members of the medical staff, which Mr. Grant always tried to avoid.

At the end of my internship, Dr. Henderson offered me a position as his assistant, conditional on my successfully graduating from Columbia in three months' time. We agreed on a salary and I would get free accommodations in the village. I was over the moon. It was the start of a career that would last a lifetime. I was 28 years old.

Olea

The three women in my life — two wives and Olea.

It was one year of celibacy, after my first wife's disappearance; and during a semester break from Columbia, I was sitting on a large sofa in my parents' living room. I heard my mother greet someone in the hallway. "Oh, hello Olea! What a nice surprise. How wonderful to see you after such a long time. David is here; come in and say hello."

Olea was my younger sister's best friend. I had not seen her in more than a decade. There she stood in the doorway of the living room. Only the face was familiar, the rest of her was all grown up. She looked very Nordic — fresh outdoor, fair complexion; long, straight blonde hair like corn silk, curious blue eyes, a turned up nose — a joyful mature face.

She was wearing the latest European fashion of the time — a mini skirt that went to the middle of her thigh. A perfectly shaped bosom with a slightly daring décollage. Having just arrived from "Swinging London," her lifestyle was the cutting edge early '60s. She was an example of the Chelsea Girl: Twiggy, Jean Shrimpton ("The Shrimp"), Kings Road, The Rolling Stones, Mary Quant. She exemplified '60s' morals and values of the age of "The Pill" and "Angry Young Men." She was "so cool."

The following day, I asked her for a date and shortly after that, another. Soon we started sharing weekends, holidays, and living together in New York City while she attended typing school (in those days, even a degree from Smith College required typing skills to enter the job market). Moreover, for most girls at the time, the only other options for employment were nursing, teaching, and sales assistants.

She unknowingly helped restore my confidence with the opposite sex. Olea showed an appreciation for me in our relationship that I had not encountered before. She had a certain experienced naivety with a young girl's inquisitiveness about everything, including sex with all its curiosity and passion. She was unintentionally suggestive and sensual. She once asked if there was an equivalent of *Playboy* magazine for women.

At the same time, she was bright and very intelligent — I admired this in a relationship. I asked for her hand in marriage. I was confident of her feelings toward me, but at the same time I knew she needed more time to live — to breathe deeper. I was very sad when she went back to Italy, but that's what lovers usually do — they go away.

Twenty-five years later, I had the opportunity of introducing mine and Dale's daughter, Eliza, to Olea. I said: "Eliza, if I had not married your mother, this is the lady I would have tried to marry." Eliza and Olea talked together for a while and then Eliza asked in the same, open naïve manner that Olea would have asked: "Why didn't you marry my father?"

Olea hesitated, looked at me and said: "Time. It wasn't the right time."

Dale

Shortly after, I had the opportunity of going to a wedding or my graduation from Columbia University. Fortuitously, I chose the wedding.

Dale's story started a long time ago, a story my father told me. Years later, Dale's mother, Corinne, confirmed it.

Dale lived just outside of Newtown. Her mother would travel regularly into the town center, going past a newly-constructed sign that read "J. Benton Egee, M.D.". She thought to herself that this must be the new doctor in town.

One day, Corinne was driving Dale and her sister, Andy, in their Ford station wagon (known to surfers now as a "woody") when suddenly the door of the car opened and Andy fell out. She was unconscious. Corinne rushed her to the new doctor's office. As they were leaving his office after the treatment, my father said:

"Funny thing, I was just reading about concussions."

That's how Dale's parents and my parents met and became lifelong friends.

I was three and Dale was five when she entered my life (see photos). We attended Mrs. Manack's nursery school together, although neither one of us has any memory of that except a photo that proves it. I do remember an occasion, however, when I was four or five. It was a cold December evening when I fell in love. My mother said to me that Dale would be passing by with her parents for a short visit. Friends often stopped by — my mother was very sociable.

I said to my mother, "I will build an igloo and Dale and I can play in it." My mother put on my "snow suit" and I spent the afternoon making, as I remember, a rather successful igloo. It had a small window but the roof kept falling in. The afternoon grew dark, but Dale's parents still hadn't arrived. My mother called me into the house to say that her parents were delayed and that it was time for my bath before dinner. By the time Dale finally arrived, I was in my pajamas, the old-fashioned kind — one single suit with snaps up the front and a flap at the back. That's when Dale finally arrived. It was not the impression I had intended to make.

Because we lived in the direction of the town center, Corinne would often stop by our house for a visit. If Dale was with her mother, she would go directly to our bedroom and open the huge built-in drawer next to my bed that was filled with comics, courtesy of a friend of my parents who worked for the publishers of DC Comics. She would sit on the floor right next to it, her legs spread straight out, with her back against the side of my bed and a pile of comics at her side. I sat beside her. Dale could read but I just looked at the pictures. It would be 20 years before I got her that close to a bed again.

Dale continued to go to the Sandy Hook school until she was 13 years old when her parents moved to Westport, Connecticut, 25 miles away. It was a fancy suburb within commuting distance of New York City. Her father was a Princeton University graduate and worked for *Life Magazine*. He rose up through the ranks of Time-Life Inc. and became head of advertising. He was tall and attractive in a Marlboro man sort of way, a lifestyle illustrated in the current TV series, Mad Men.

Although I didn't see Dale again until I was 28, I would get periodic reports from my mother, who told me how Dale graduated from a private school in Connecticut, how she then went on to Rosemont College in Pennsylvania, and how she left college to continue her art studies in Florence, Italy. I remember thinking how lucky she was — to be able to travel, to live in a foreign country. How daring. She must be pretty smart. Other reports continued about how she came back to America and married a very successful advertising executive. Dale was a patient of my father's. He delivered two of her three children. She and her new husband became friends with my parents and, on occasion, played bridge together.

I continued to hear about their new and very modern butterfly-winged house. And how Dale studied landscape gardening and started a successful career in the area. My mother used to speak about what style she had in decorating her house, how wonderful she looked, and what a great cook she was. In my mind, Dale had become a super woman and pretty high on any pedestal.

It was 1966, and four days before Christmas; the cards had been posted, the presents were under the tree and a large Christmas family dinner was being planned. Suddenly, at the age of 32, Dale's husband Peter died in his sleep, leaving Dale a young widow with three children.

Dale's first port of call was my father. He arranged for an autopsy to definitively determine the cause of Peter's tragic death. He had Arterial Sclerotic Cardiovascular Disease in which an artery wall thickens. It can, as in Peter's case, go unrecognized, manifesting no symptoms.

A few months passed. The daughter of a mutual friend of both Dale's parents and mine was getting married in June on the day of my graduation from Colombia, and we were invited to the wedding. After six months of widowhood, Dale felt able to accept the invitation. Preferring a good wedding to Columbia University's graduation ceremony, I also decided to accept.

The bride's father, Robert "Ray" Rich, was at the time the CEO of Alcoa Aluminium Company. And, true to his name: very, very rich. He had, for example, his own railway car, which he could have attached to the New York, New Haven and Hartford railway whenever he wanted to travel along the eastern seaboard.

The wedding took place at their home on Martha's Vineyard off the coast of Massachusetts. It was spectacular with the ferry from the mainland to Martha's Vineyard chartered specifically for the event.

An airplane circled the ferry, trailing a band of pink mist. We walked from the dock to the church service and the reception followed. A late lunch with dancing and entertainment followed late in the evening; then we headed back to the mainland.

My mother and Dale's mother agreed that Dale and I fell in love that weekend, and in the next few weeks Dale and I came to agree with them. My parents and I picked Dale up at home to take to the wedding. My heart lifted when I first saw her. She was not walking, but skipping down the long shallow steps through the garden that led to her house. She wore a pink men's shirt, tight blue jeans, "Capezio" shoes, and no jewelry except for two small gold earrings (we were to change into our glad rags for the wedding later). To me, she was Grace Kelly and Katharine Hepburn combined, with a dash of Jane Russell. She was slim with an intellectually-sized bosom. Casual, breezy, and confident.

I think I fell in love at that exact moment, despite my mother's later comment: "But she has no bum!" She had a natural elegance and refinement that had been honed by her two-year European experience. She was an avid reader, extremely intelligent, and spoke Italian and French. I envied her curiosity and understanding of cultural and intellectual pursuits. Her confidence and her enthusiasm for new ideas spilled over. Dale provided me with the assurance that I could take on a new life with a new wife and three children all at the same time.

We relished in the newfound attraction to one another and acted as though we were 15 years younger, making love whenever and wherever we could. I put my arm around her while driving my Oldsmobile convertible. Dale was always a little concerned that she wasn't acting like a responsible mother of three children and once went all the way to New York for confession because she was afraid to go to the local parish. We married in a small church in Georgetown, Connecticut, on September 6, 1967, during a Labor Day weekend, and honeymooned in the Red Lion Hotel in New Hampshire. We had to return in time for the children to go to school on Tuesday morning.

Kindergarten, Sandy Hook School, Newtown, CT, 1943. David, second row, squinting; Dale, top row, middle, standing.

David holding the Rumsey Hall prize, 1952.

My Mother and Sister, on the day my father opened his medical practice in 1936.

Assembling my Erector set, age 8.

Rumsey Hall Hockey Team, 1952. David Egee, bottom row, extreme right.

Egee Family, Beirut, 1972.

Dale Egee, Beirut, 1972.

David Egee (center), with Dean of Johns Hopkins Medical School and the President of the American Hospital Association, 1974.

Aerial View of Olmet Courtyard, Olmet, France

My father and I, Olmet, 1985.

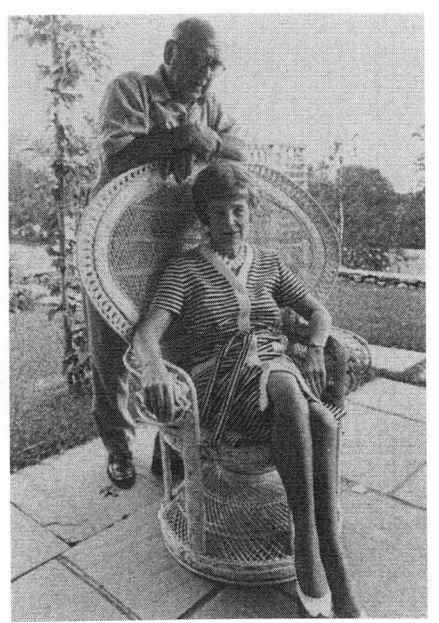

Dr. J. Benton Egee, my father, with my mother, Gladys. Newtown, CT, 1976.

Dale and I with our children: (l. to r.) Tony, Eliza, Adam, Cece. London, England, 1980.

David Egee stands to left of the Wali of Nizwah, surrounded by his entourage, 1970.

David Egee, Director of the American University Hospital in Beirut, standing in the hospital lobby, 1975.

David Egee, Managing Director of Dalecare, standing in front of Newbury Dalecare nursing home, Newbury, England, May 1988.

The Middle East

Four months after Dale and I married, her parents agreed to look after the children so that we could take a proper two-week honeymoon. We both wanted someplace warm and foreign. When Dale was an art student in Florence, she had travelled to some parts of the Middle East and loved it. Her parents had dear friends John and Isabel Fistere, living in Beirut. So we spent a week in Morocco then went on to visit the Fisteres in Beirut.

Beirut

John Fistere was an advisor and speechwriter for King Hussein of Jordan. He wrote the famous speech about defining Israeli borders that the King delivered at the United Nations Assembly in 1967. He and his wife knew everybody who was anybody in the city and they organized a dinner party for us. The guests included the American ambassador, a member of the board of trustees of the American University, and the dean of the medical school at the university. The dean, in turn, introduced me to the director of the American University Hospital (AUH) the following day.

We met and got along well. He was in the midst of a huge building program, similar to one I was working on in New Jersey. He offered me a job as assistant director. In April

1968, Dale, and now four children and I moved from our rural farmhouse in Flemington, New Jersey, to the middle of Beirut, Lebanon. That was the start of the best seven years of our lives as a family. Dale often said, "Those seven years were magical."

For Dale and me, working and living abroad was romantic, exciting, and we thought even heroic. It set us aside from the ordinary. We were both keen to live overseas for a period of time. Little did we realize it would last a lifetime.

In 1862, American missionaries in Lebanon and Syria, headed by Dr. Daniel Bliss, were asked to start a "college of higher education that would include medical training." The college, known as the Syrian Protestant College, accepted its first class of 16 students in 1866 and in 1867, the college started its medical school. In 1905, it opened a hospital. The State of New York granted it a charter in 1920, and the name was changed to the American University of Beirut, which became a center of learning for people throughout the Middle East. To give some sense of its impact in the region, 19 alumni of the university were delegates to the signing of the United Nations Charter in New York in 1945. Its graduates served as presidents, prime ministers, members of parliaments, ambassadors, governors of central banks, presidents of universities, business leaders, engineers, doctors, nurses, and teachers.

The university's funding depended on various Middle Eastern countries, companies, government grants, and private donors. Corporations such as Bechtel Construction Company and Mobil Oil funded the creation of the College of Engineering in the early 1940s and 1960s; the United States' Department of International Development became a major supporter. During this time, Arab countries, particularly the oil-rich ones, donated large sums of money towards various buildings and programs. Dr. Samuel Kirkwood, with whom I had the honor of working, became the president of the American University of Beirut in 1963 and remained so until the early years of the civil war, which started in 1975. Before that, he had worked with the US government in Iran, heading up a large construction project for countrywide hospitals. Dr. Kirkwood's interest in medical affairs enabled him to obtain a $20 million grant from the US government for the redevelopment of the medical facilities at the hospital. The project involved the creation of a 400-bed hospital, with ancillary services included. The grant also allowed for the creation of a postgraduate medical training center, a new medical library, and a school of nursing. Construction started in 1964 and the project was completed in 1970. When it opened its doors that year, it was to be the newest, most modern medical facility in the entire Middle East. Because of the quality of the medical staff and its affiliation with teaching hospitals in America, the hospital developed a reputation for excellence throughout the Middle East.

All members of the medical staff had a minimum of four years postgraduate training in various hospitals throughout the United States. For example, Dr. Roger Akel was on duty in the Parkland Hospital in Dallas, Texas, in 1963. He was the first physician to see President Kennedy when he was brought to the emergency room. The head of the department of surgery, Dr. Ibrahim Dagher, was trained under Dr. DeBakey, the renowned heart surgeon. The hospital was the first port of call for any American working in embassies throughout the Middle East.

My job as assistant director was a newly created position and was the result of the multimillion-dollar hospital construction project. When I arrived, the basic construction work was nearing completion. After the first year in my new position, we began to equip, furnish, and operate the new outpatient department. At the same time, a second position for assistant director was vacant because the incumbent had completed his three-year contract and wanted to return to America. Tom Clarke, a man my age, was appointed. He had arrived a month before me and had established a very good working relationship with our boss, Ed Stockman, the hospital director. I realized immediately that if anything happened to our boss, we would both be competing for his job. I had an office in the executive area of the hospital. I also had a field office in the new hospital, which was where most of my time was spent. Meanwhile, Tom Clarke worked closely with Ed on continuing operations in the existing facility. When Ed left for a two-week holiday, he appointed Tom as acting director. I feared that Tom was already being groomed for Ed's position, which would become vacant in two years, when Ed planned to return to America after completing his contract. I talked about my concerns with Dale, worrying about what might happen, and imagining Tom Clarke as my boss. As usual, her response was, "Don't be silly, they're going to select you."

We were extremely happy living in Beirut and were there for the long term. Being responsible for the new facility gave me an opportunity to have regular contact with the dean of the medical faculties, who reported directly to the president of the university. I sometimes accompanied him on meetings with the president. I also got to know the heads of the various medical departments, helped them move into the new facility, discussed with them their required changes, and the procedures we wanted to install in the new hospital. Not surprisingly, their main concern was the size and the location of the department heads' offices. I was enjoying my work fully and was confident of fitting in with the local staff as well as the local population itself. I was surprised by the progress I was making in learning Arabic. Although the hospital and university were run in English, efforts to use Arabic were appreciated by everybody, from the laundry workers to the president's office.

One of my earlier tasks was to receive 15 large sea containers filled with equipment, furnishings, and initial supplies for the hospital. Because the US government funded the project, everything had to be manufactured and shipped by American-owned companies, which included everything from surgical equipment to visitors' chairs, curtains, and telephones.

I had to put together a team of local laborers to unload the containers. Most were peasants from Syria or Palestinians living in refugee camps. Out of about 15 men, one emerged as a natural leader. He was bald and had a well-trimmed grey beard. The others called him Hajj because he had made the pilgrimage to Mecca. He wore the title well. He wore baggy shalwar trousers; a dirty, loose-fitting shirt; and plastic sandals. Today, he might be described as looking like a stereotypical Taliban combatant.

I liked him and appointed him my informal foreman. He could not speak a word of English, which helped immensely in my language training. The hospital staff was impressed by my progress and some said I spoke Arabic with a slight Syrian accent. I learned about some of their customs regarding their prayer times, when they ate, their rest periods, holy days, and other work habits to which I would otherwise not have been exposed. I learned the difference between Shiites, Sunnis, Alawites, and Druze; and that was just on the Muslim side. In Lebanon, you also had to learn the difference between Maronite and Greek Orthodox, and just plain old Roman Catholics. To a westerner, all mosques look alike, but Hajj taught me how to tell the difference between Shiite and Sunni mosques.

One day, Hajj came to me and asked if he and his colleagues could have a place to live on site. He asked if they could live in the huge surplus drainage culverts that were stored off to one corner of the site. Before I knew it, a small hamlet had been created. On one occasion soon after, my boss Ed passed by (he had a strange lack of interest in the new project) and casually remarked, "Egee, that's going to be your responsibility to see that this is dismantled when we finish." I would have two more years of experience with local culture before I had to execute the order.

When the time came, the laborers could see that work was coming to a halt, but they were reluctant to leave. I went to the head of our maintenance department, Jaha Bolous, and asked him how I was going to get rid of the campsite. A look of concern crossed his face for just a second. Then he said, "We'll wait until their holiday when they go back to Syria for their weekend. Then I'll get a tractor and a couple of men."

When they came back from their break on Monday, the little community was gone. Jaha tried to assuage my guilt: "Mr. David, all of modern Beirut was built just the same way as this hospital is being built — by peasants and Palestinian refugees. It's all of the same. They stay until they are pushed off. The Palestinians go back to their camps; the Syrians back to Damascus until they find another construction project. Don't worry, you're not in New Jersey anymore." It was the custom and my job was not to change the culture but to get the hospital ready to open.

In 1968, the university celebrated its centenary. The university's administrative structure and its place in the community was pretty much the same as when Daniel Bliss first started it. But when Dr. Kirkwood, the president, arrived in 1963, he felt it was time to reexamine its role within an entirely new economic age, one that witnessed the price of oil rising from $0.50 cents to $12 a barrel; and a new political age, in which the American government played a much greater role.

So much was happening — the Israeli occupation of Palestine, huge amounts of oil wealth in Lebanon, increasing numbers of refugees, volatile political conditions in neighboring countries, the ever-increasing financial involvement of the US government with the university. This new social order had a dramatic influence on the university. In light of that, the US government provided a grant to carry out a review of the existing administrative structure.

A new administrative hierarchy was created. Although this new hierarchy would impact the hospital indirectly, it influenced my position directly. A position, vice president for administration, was created and Dwight Monnier, a former Department of Defence (DOD) bigwig, was appointed. Until he arrived, the hospital was autonomous from the rest of the university — it was the biggest part of the university and generated income for the Medical School.

When a new position is created at the highest levels of any organization, people below feel threatened. What was going to happen to each person's little turf? Monnier's changes meant that the hospital's administrative functions would move from the dean's happy office to his. That included me. I thought change was a good thing — it offered new opportunities. But to Stockman, it was a threat.

Monnier was followed around by a retired colonel with a clipboard and assisted by a retired general from the Army Corps of Engineers, who oversaw the actual construction of the new hospital. I spoke with them regularly on behalf of Ed Stockman, who did not like either the former general or colonel.

As my day was spent wholly involved with the new facility, Ed Stockman and Tom Clarke continued working together at the old one. Tom's office adjoined Ed's. They had lunch every day in his office and played cards with two other people after lunch. Ed, his wife and daughter became an important part of Tom's social life. Every weekend they went together to the university's private beach, a social center of the entire university.

Ed reported directly to the Dean of the Medical Faculties and to the President of the University. He saw the new university structure headed by Vice President Monnier as infringing on his responsibilities and a threat to his position. The more he minimized his contact with the new vice president, the better. One day, I was called to Monnier's office, which was on the executive floor of the university and closest to the president's. He said he wanted to ask me some questions to get "a full feel" of the hospital situation and the progress of the move to new facilities. Finally, he said, "Egee, tell me, and please understand that this is a highly confidential meeting and strictly off the record…"

Sitting next to him was the Colonel, his ever-present deputy. He stared at me with a clipboard in his hand and a pen in his mouth.

"Tell me," Monnier repeated.

"Yes," I replied. I had been in his office on other occasions, but always with my boss and others.

"I need to know if Ed Stockman and Tom Clarke are homosexuals. I need to know if they are having a relationship with one another." He paused. "Let me remind you again that this is a confidential meeting."

I was flabbergasted. This was completely "off the wall." I was totally unprepared. I knew they were concerned about delays in the opening of the hospital and about the actual move into the facility, but I never anticipated a concern such as this.

From my meetings with Dr. Monnier and from my own understanding of his character, I was certain that he was not a man who would tolerate deviant behavior in members of his "team." I didn't want to see my boss fired. Not yet, at least. I was sitting on the top floor of the first and largest structure built here in 1866. It was a stone building in colonial Mediterranean style, and the office was large with high ceilings and a tiled floor. A ceiling fan turned slowly. This was the epicenter of power for the university, with the offices of the most senior people and where the most important and critical decisions were made. And I was being asked if my boss is a homosexual.

I knew that there were rumors to that effect. I knew that Tom and Ed spent time together: They would get their hair cut together and both had it dyed prematurely grey. They used to go Dr. Harukian's office to have their prostates massaged. When I looked at Tom in mild surprise, he told me how good it felt and how relaxing it was. I knew that Tom lived in the same apartment block as Ed and spent many evenings in his apartment. But I also knew that Ed had a lovely wife and a charming daughter. And knowing that nothing in college hall was confidential, at last I spoke.

"I really don't know. I know it's rumored that they're gay, but I never saw them touch one another and I never saw anything that would confirm without a doubt that they were homosexual or having a relationship." I knew that Monnier wanted me to give him a simple yes. I, too, wanted to be a part of his team. But I really did *not* want Ed to be fired. At least not yet.

A few months later, Tom Clarke and Ed Stockman resigned. Obviously, I never discussed their resignations, but Ed told me he had been offered the directorship of the La Hoya Medical Centre in San Diego, California, and Tom had accepted the directorship of a nursing home facility in Manhattan, New York City. I was appointed acting director. The president, Dr. Kirkwood, called me to his office. He said I was doing a very good job and was particularly pleased to see that the medical staff spoke highly of my support, and that I was working well with Monnier. He added that the selection committee was appointing a new director.

He thought that I was too young for the permanent position and that they would be looking for a more experienced individual. But he hoped I would continue as acting director of the hospital in the meantime. I thought to myself, *I'm 32 years old. Gaddafi has just taken over Libya and he is only 29.* I kept my mouth shut. After nearly a year, a candidate from John Hopkins University Medical Centre in Maryland was appointed, but he withdrew his application at the last minute because his wife was diagnosed with cancer, and he wanted to remain in the States. Dr. Riyad Tabara, head of the department of medicine and a member of the selection committee, suggested to Dr. Kirkwood that he appoint me as the new director.

The dean of the medical faculties called me to his office and outlined how the new management structure would be implemented. He made it clear that while I was formally responsible directly to him, I would informally work with the new office of the vice president for administration while the new overall administrative structure was being implemented. I would also work closely with Dr. Nasif, the director of the medical school. He added that he was quite tired of everyone trying to protect their own turf in this period of change, and hoped that I would work successfully with the administration and medical staff.

I may not have become the director because I was a great administrator, but I did learn that it helps to be in the right place at the right time.

I had two assistants. Both were graduates of the American University of Beirut and both were sent by the hospital to get their graduate degree in Hospital Administration. We worked together through my entire seven-year period in Lebanon.

Machiavellian by nature, my first assistant, Salam Reyes, had a quiet, subdued manner. Always probing for the other's motivations, his was not the commonly perceived image of the laid-back southern Mediterranean inhabitant. Nevertheless, he did have a sense of humor, but you had to dig deep to find it. A few months after my departure, Salam accepted the directorship of a hospital in Beirut with an excellent reputation.

My other assistant, Munther Kuzoli, provided the perfect balance for Salam. Outgoing and sociable, he was a good front man when dealing with the hospital and medical staffs. Except for a brief period in Saudi Arabia, Munther became the director of the hospital and remained so until his recent retirement. Heading up the hospital throughout the 15-year civil war was an incredible achievement and, as luck would have it, he survived the experience. He lived on the university campus believing it to be more secure for him and his young family. The President of the University and the Dean of Students were both shot and killed. During that period, the hospital was obviously not a safe or secure place.

Another key member of my staff was the Director of Nursing, Miss Carter. She was 55, but with her cosmetic surgery "tucks," she looked like an attractive 40-year-old. She had been director of nursing during the five years that Ed Stockman was director and during the tenures of two previous hospital directors, as well.

Ed Stockman worked around her; the medical staff worked against her; and her own staff, being the highest paid nurses in Lebanon, simply put up with her. She directed from the top down rather from the bottom up. She never wore the nurses' uniform, nor did her two assistants. She was never seen on the nursing wards of the hospital; she delegated that work to others. She led by intimidation.

I was once told that a strategy for a new director in any organization should be to make an immediate decision that will have an early impact on the whole organization. The more dramatic, the higher the profile, the better. Miss Carter presented just that opportunity so I fired her.

Soon after, Dr. Tabara, Chief of the Department of Medicine, passed by my office. In the Middle East, colleagues never request an appointment; they just pass by assuming your door is always open and you will be in. "Congratulations, David. Very good," he said with his usual sneaky smile. "She's been here fifteen years, nearly as long as the Dean."

Doctor Najib Abu Haidar, head of the outpatient department, came by my office and said, "Egee, you are *al louli fi Teez el nimr*." I asked what that meant. "It's an Arabic expression meaning 'you are the pearl in the tiger's ass.' And, of course, nobody touches the tiger's ass."

The director of the medical school also walked past my door with a comment. Usually, Dr. Nasif was a man who communicated as if giving a lecture rather than having a conversation. This time it was different. "Well, she was finally forced out," he said. "You finally got rid of the dean's girlfriend."

I had no idea. I had never heard any rumors, and I had no reason to suspect. It was never mentioned between us. The dean knew by my actions that I knew nothing and the only reference he ever made was, "I understand you got rid of Miss Carter."

Spies and Terrorists

In 1968, fighting in Vietnam peaked after the Tet offensive and American forces were beginning to withdraw. Journalists, newscasters, and photographers were casting about for a new theatre of operation and almost as if scripted by TV news, three airplanes were hijacked and taken to an isolated airstrip in Jordan in September 1970. It had been organized by the Popular Front for the Liberation of Palestine (PFLP). The world media packed up and moved from Vietnam to Lebanon. The PFLP, headed by George Habash, and the Fatah, headed by Yasser Arafat, became household names in world news. The Palestinian-Israeli conflict was a headline story and has remained so till today.

The American University Hospital in Beirut (AUB hospital) also became a player. We provided the best medical care for all the participants in this phenomenally robust city. If US government employees anywhere in the Middle East required medical attention, the AUB hospital was the first port of call. Major political figures, heads of state, their advisors, media figures and members of the upper strata of the Lebanese population came to us.

One day, Dr. Samir Alami, originally from Palestine and a graduate of the medical school, asked if he could see me for a few minutes. Samir was a pathologist and head of the clinical laboratories within the hospital. It was unusual for him to call and ask for a meeting because the practice, as I said earlier, was for doctors to just drop by for a chat. He outlined for me the plight of the Palestinian people at the hands of the Israelis and the events that had led to the current situation. He told me about Fatah and its founders. He told me about the early raids on Israel made by Arafat's small commando army. The army was created in the hope that it would be able to get back the land that was occupied by Israel after the 1967 war and beyond those borders as prescribed and agreed to by the UN.

Samir mentioned the battle of Karameh, where 150 commandos were killed. He explained that some of Fatah's fighters were badly wounded. Could the most seriously wounded have access to some of our teaching hospital beds?

He assured me that all the patients would be treated by trainee doctors and the exercise would be of teaching value. He explained that the Lebanese government hospitals would not accept such patients because they were Palestinian and so they could not be admitted for political reasons. Arafat's organization was not yet well-funded enough to provide medical care for the wounded. I was aware that Samir's request had political overtones. It would have been easy to say no, but I secretly wanted to be involved.

I told him I would like to help, but first I wanted to speak with Dr. Riad Tabara to see that there would be no repercussions. Dr. Tabara was a wise man. Older than most of the staff, he was the first Lebanese doctor to run the Department of Medicine. All previous department heads had been American. He told me that Samir had already spoken with him. He felt it important that Samir's request be cleared with my office. He told me that Samir came from an old well-established Palestinian family. His brother was now the head of a Palestinian bank and a significant contributor to the cause — as well as to the university.

Dr. Tabara said he felt confident that the medical staff would not object. He was smiling and had a twinkle in his eye. It was the sort of look that two young boys give each other when they are about to do something a little naughty. "Egee," he said, "why don't you negotiate with Arafat to get us something we need besides teaching patients?"

"You mean blood donations?"

He nodded. I was about to leave his office when he added, "Egee, I haven't talked to the administration about it, but if you do this, you have the backing of the medical staff. I don't think you will have to worry about your job."

I called Samir the next day and he was in my office in a shot. I told him of my conversation with Dr. Tabara. We were to get 25 units of blood for every admission. "You can negotiate that with Yasser yourself," said Samir. "He's in my office now." I tried to look cool and unflappable, but I'm sure that the blood draining from my face gave me away.

Arafat came to my office in what was to become his familiar outfit: military fatigues. But he wore a military hat rather than the now well-known *keffiyeh*, or Palestinian headscarf. He had two Parker pens clipped to his breast pocket, canvas shoes, and was accompanied by two civilians in dark blue suits. Dr. Alami introduced us. Arafat had a very easy manner. He was not pompous and he did not act in a particularly military fashion. He appeared a little shy and unassuming. He spoke gently and had a habit of answering questions with another question. I thought naively that if the Israelis had come to my office and met him by chance, they might have been able to come to an agreement.

Samir introduced the reason for the meeting and Arafat agreed that for each admission he would provide 25 units of blood. Samir interjected that Arafat understood that the blood would not necessarily be reserved for just his people.

As the meeting came to an end, I thought it would be safe to say that if they wounded an Israeli soldier I expected them to bring him to the hospital, too.

"But, of course," he said. I wasn't so sure.

The early admissions were chaotic. The volunteer commandos insisted on coming to the emergency room in at least three open jeeps with sirens blaring. The commandos were in full uniform with Kalashnikovs at the ready. They jumped out of their vehicles and presented their bare arms for blood donations to the receptionist. It was all very macho. I'm sure the receptionist was scared to death. The program ran without incident and as time went by, Arafat's army grew in size, became better funded, and his cause more popular. His army was able to treat more of their own casualties by themselves in their own facilities. The doctors were volunteers, including some of our own graduates.

It was sometimes said in Beirut, "Everyone was a spy or knew a spy." Being cynical by nature, I was never able to take this spy business seriously. I never took the accusation of being a spy myself very seriously, either. I thought of it as banter, a "Hardy Boys" sort of thing. Besides, the spies that we knew were without exception very intelligent, inquisitive (I guess you have to be in that line of work), and educated people. They specialized in lower level stuff, informants, surveillance, anonymous cells collecting fragmented information, setting up "objective files," and monitoring people's daily movements — a far cry from the glamorous world of espionage novels. It seemed like pretty innocent stuff, but I was intrigued by it.

One day, Samir again asked if we could have a short meeting. He came to my office to discuss Dr. George Habash, a graduate of the American University medical school and founder of the Popular Front for the Liberation of Palestine (PFLP), the organization responsible for blowing up three planes in the middle of the Jordanian desert. He'd had what was assumed to be a heart attack.

Samir told me that his doctors wanted to admit him as a private patient and asked if I could somehow arrange special security for him. He explained that it would be very helpful if his admission could remain strictly confidential. He would be admitted under a false name. We discussed this with the head of the department of cardiology and the new head of the nursing department. It was agreed that by dressing Habash's female soldiers in our own hospital's volunteer uniforms, some additional security could then be provided. The "volunteers" would position themselves at the entrance to his suite.

The next morning I received a phone call from a friend who worked in the economic section of the American Embassy. The pretext for his call was to tell me that he happened to be in the area and wanted to discuss our plans for the weekend, when we were supposed to go skiing. When he came to my office, he got right to the point. "I understand you have George Habash in the hospital," he said. I suppose I should have suspected that he was CIA, but I honestly did not.

"So you are not an economist after all?"

"Well, not full time." He wanted to speak to one of the consulting doctors about Habash's health. I explained to him that I did not want to appear uncooperative or unhelpful and asked him to respect my position and the role of the hospital, which I wanted to preserve. He did not push it further, but we never went skiing again nor did we have any further contact.

John Niffy and his wife Jane were also friends. He, too, worked in the American Embassy, in the "political section." Dale and I and our friends assumed that he was a spy. Having been to our home for various dinners, he knew that Dale was a very good hostess. She was skilled at organizing such occasions and mixing various people, circulating to see everyone was well attended to. John asked if we could organize a party and if he could bring a couple of "friends" from the Russian Embassy. He explained that the Russian he wanted to talk to was married to a gynecologist. He thought if I invited a couple of gynecologists from our hospital staff, this would give her the opportunity to meet people of her same profession and give him the chance to establish further contact with the Russian in question.

When I proposed this idea to Dale she was not pleased. In fact, she was vehemently opposed to the idea. "Why do you want to have the CIA and the Russian KGB using our apartment to discuss their filthy business? Why are you so keen on this; why do you want to get involved?"

How could I explain to her that I thought dipping into the lives and activities of the KGB and CIA might be interesting? It may even be a little bit of fun. Needless to say, my spying days were over.

Another time, I received a telephone call late at night from one of our emergency room doctors. He said there was an emergency admission. Members of the Sitash (a special branch of the police), a doctor from the Egyptian Embassy, and our nurses and staff physicians were gathered in the emergency room. Could I come right over? When I arrived, I quickly learned that the patient in question was a member of the Saudi royal family. I was not impressed because I knew the Saudi king had some 3,000 pampered family members living in various playground cities across Europe and the Middle East. What did impress me a little, however, was that he was the nephew of the king, of which there were only about 250.

The young man had been at the popular, noisy Cave du Roi nightclub. It was inhabited by well-connected, spoiled young Lebanese and an array of foreign journalist friends. It seemed that Prince Faisal bin Musaid got into a brawl and was stabbed in the back, resulting in what was thought to be a severed spinal cord. Pressure was put upon me from various quarters to treat him as a VIP patient. We placed him in a special ward.

He was a young man of 27. Spoiled, aggressive, an alcoholic, and extremely wealthy; all the elements that make for trouble. I found out later that when he attended the University of Colorado, he was caught consuming and selling LSD, and he was also frequently drunk.

His stay in the hospital was a nightmare. According to an Egyptian-trained doctor, his hangers-on brought drinks and prostitutes to his room to "help with his therapy and improve his morale." One evening, things got rowdy so my assistant went to the room to quiet the situation. He was literally thrown out by Joe Malone, a "special projects director" who was part of the "new AUB restructuring program." Joe Malone was reliably reported to be sponsored by the CIA.

Naturally, I complained to the dean. He asked that I remain patient and handle the situation as best I could. I even called the US ambassador to see if we could expedite his transfer to another hospital or back to Saudi Arabia. In the end, although he walked unsteadily, the prince recovered some mobility. His high living days at the *Cave du Roi* were over. He was finally discharged and returned to Saudi Arabia.

On March 25, 1975, while staying in the Intercontinental Hotel in Tehran, I was reading the telexes coming off the machine in the lobby and discovered that King Faisal had been shot and killed by his nephew Faisal bin Musaid, who had joined with a Kuwaiti delegation waiting to meet the King. When the King bent down to speak to Prince Musaid, the latter pulled out a pistol and shot the King twice in the head. Three months later, the Prince was beheaded in a public square in Riyadh.

The high profile of AUH throughout the region put me in the privileged position of being called upon by other Middle East health ministries and corporations to give advice, provide consultancy services, and offer opinions about hospital operations.

Again, it was not my ingenuity that earned me the opportunity to travel throughout the region, but simply the circumstances in which I found myself. My trips were always in the name of the hospital and, therefore, there was no financial gain on my part. But I did get tremendous personal joy from these visits. I knew my presence in the area helped to promote the hospital and the university. I was enhancing the hospital's reputation as a regional provider of services. I was "spreading the gospel."

Once I visited Saudi Arabia at the request of the Deputy Minister of Health. We had met by chance when his wife required admission for a minor procedure. He invited me to come and visit his office as his guest for a few days.

His office was on the second floor. In those days, there were no elevators in ministerial offices, or if there were, they didn't work. So the minister's office was always on the first floor and the deputy's on the second. The lower you were in the chain of command, the higher your office. He said the ministry had contracted a German company to build and equip 10 hospitals, all alike. These were completed in 1968 and five years later, they still were not occupied. I visited one of them. It was a strange sight. They were all situated in open areas outside small cities. When I visited, sand had blown across the car park and was piling up against the buildings themselves. The main drive was obscured by sand. The front door had to be shoved open. The reception area was covered with dust. The operating theatres were covered with a light film of sand: a 150-bed hospital, lying empty with only the sound of wind. It was spooky and sad.

"Mr. David, I can find a hundred companies to build me a hospital, but I don't have a single Saudi who can run one," the Deputy Minister of Health said to me. He explained that building and equipping hospitals was "an excellent business, particularly with the 25 percent commissions that local businessmen received." But running and staffing these facilities was simply not possible. The Saudi Arabian government was unable to deal with the situation. Hotels, airlines, highways, schools, the Army — they were all managed by westerners and staffed by what were called "third-country nationals."

"We Saudis must begin by doing this ourselves," he said.

"We couldn't run your hospitals at this time, but we could certainly start training your people to run them," I replied. It was a throwaway remark, something to please him. He took me seriously.

"I want a proposal in three months," he said. I laughed.

"No, no, I'm serious. If you can create such a program, Saudi Arabia's Ministry of Health will pay for it. All I want at this moment is a proposal. Just assure me that these students will be able to abide by their cultural values and religious beliefs." He reiterated that the Ministry of Health would cover all costs associated with creating the program, including the building of any necessary facilities.

What an exciting project! What an academic challenge! What a gift to the university! Flying back to Lebanon, I was over the moon. But I also knew I was completely out of my depth. I had no time or skill to develop a proposal on such a scale. Nevertheless, I had a gut feeling the university could. In fact, the American University of Beirut was in the best position to offer training based on the specific needs of their country. No other institution in the region was as uniquely placed as ours.

I was not worried about selling the idea to the Dean or President of the University. They would surely accept this undertaking once they understood that Saudi Arabia would cover all costs. My worry had more to do with: Who the hell would produce such a proposal?

As soon as I got back to my office, I described to Salam what had happened on my trip. I asked who he thought we could get to head the project. He had the answer before I'd finished speaking.

"Speak to Dr. Haddad," he said. "He's a graduate of the medical school and has recently come back from the United States with a master's in public health." I had sat in on a few meetings with Dr. Haddad. He said very little. He would listen to the speaker and observe others carefully. When views and comments were being offered, the Dean would invariably ask him what he thought. In three sentences, he would summarize what the others had taken ten minutes to discuss. I always looked forward to his responses.

As I spoke to Dr. Haddad about the project, he became more and more convinced of our possible success, not only in gaining ministerial approval, but in our ability to develop a hospital administration program.

The proposal was written and presented as if it had come from the Dean himself. In fact, the Dean had no interest in the Saudis or Saudi Arabia. Frankly, he had no interest in the Arab world in general, and Saudi Arabia in particular. I know of only one occasion when he travelled to Saudi Arabia, and that was with Dr. Haddad and me. The Dean was a heavy drinker, categorically unsympathetic to Arab drinking laws and beliefs.

The proposal itself was a work of genius. It would become a model for future projects that Dr. Haddad presided over throughout the Arab world. He created similar training programs for students in Bahrain.

While developing the proposal, Dr. Haddad used to invite me to join him on the numerous trips he made to the Kingdom. I was flattered that he wanted to include me, but I had to admit to him that I was really not very useful. He said, "David, your presence is important. To the Saudi Deputy Minister, you are the hospital and the university. You flatter them by your presence. I give the project its medical legitimacy and assure the ministry of our sensitivity to the local culture. Besides, they like your blue eyes and fair complexion."

I enjoyed accompanying him. I rather liked running after the millions of Saudi dollars and dipping into the excitement of the commercial world. It was a contrast to the serenity of the academic world. We both had the idea that we were not trying to sell the Saudis something; we believed we were genuinely helping the Kingdom to improve itself.

In 1971, my three-year contract at the Hospital expired. If Dale and I decided to remain for a second tour of duty, which we did, we were entitled to a return trip to America plus a 30-day sabbatical to be spent in our home of record. In our case, that was Connecticut. But we preferred to spend our 30 days travelling around the world. I went to the Dean to discuss the definition of "return to your home of record." He said that, to him, the spirit of the sabbatical was to renew our family contacts back in America and our allegiance to the United States.

"We want to be sure that you don't 'go native,' " he said. But the rule did not necessarily apply to the family. They would be given the round-trip fare in any event. He added that if he was asked by the president or the vice-president of the university where David Egee was, he wanted to be able to look them in the eye and say, "David has returned to America for his home leave."

"As far as I'm concerned, how you go and how long it takes you to get there is your own affair," he said. I think we understood one another.

We shipped the children to the two sets of grandparents and decided to travel. We visited Afghanistan, Nepal, India, Hong Kong, and Japan. When we reached Japan, I went on to the US and Dale went back to Beirut via Sri Lanka.

Just as we touched down in Hong Kong, the stewardess called over the speaker system, "Will Mr. Egee please identify himself?" I thought Dr. Kirkwood had found out where we were and that I was in trouble. Then the stewardess handed me a note, indicating that I would be met by a Mr. Louis and a Mr. Glan, one of whom would be a tall man in a red jacket.

They were there when we came through Customs. Before even greeting us, Mr. Louis said, "Don't worry; no bad news."

He explained that he and his colleague had flown all the way from Waltham, Massachusetts, to meet with me. They were from Raytheon, an arms manufacturer.

At the time, Raytheon was in the fifth year of a 25-year contract to supply the Saudis with Hawk missiles, upgrade their systems, as well as establish a training program to enable the Saudis to assume full responsibility at the end of the contract. (As of today, Raytheon's Hawk missile contract has kept them in Saudi Arabia for 44 years. For one reason or another, I assume the Saudis are still unable to operate the systems by themselves.)

Following the American business ethic of constant growth and expansion, the company wanted to respond to a Saudi Ministry of Defense request for proposals to build and operate a small 50-bed hospital for Raytheon and Saudi employees connected with the program. Of course, Raytheon's expertise was in killing people, not in treating them. But that didn't hold the Raytheon Corporation back. A preliminary proposal had to be submitted within 30 days, which explained the urgency of meeting with me.

"How did you know I was in Hong Kong?" I asked.

"Your assistant, Salam, told us that you are on your home leave and that your travel agent was Malikian Travel on Hamra Street. They happen to be our travel agents, as well," he said with a smile.

When I returned to Beirut a "letter of understanding" was signed between the hospital and Raytheon. But, however profitable our dealings with Raytheon could have been, the question of aligning ourselves with an arms' manufacturer remained a problem. We submitted the proposal, but did not pursue the matter any further.

Olmet

In the summer months, particularly August and September, Beirut was a very hot (40-42C) and humid (100 percent) place to live and work. Even though I liked the Mediterranean summers, those two months were the most unbearable.

For one month of the year, we wanted to rest and do nothing. We had a romantic dream of a small maintenance-free house, made of stone. "You can't take it with you" is a phrase that becomes a lot more relevant as you grow older. We wanted to buy a small place somewhere in Italy or France for our summer holidays, a modest house that we could lock up at the end of a few weeks and come back to the following year.

Our first choice was Italy because Dale went to art school in Florence. She had loved the experience, the people, the food, and the language when she was young, single, and beautiful. We took a two-week trip to Tuscany in 1973 with the sole objective of purchasing our dream house. We failed. The following summer, friends invited us to spend two weeks with them in southwest France, about 40 kilometers from Montpellier. We looked around, but found nothing that was just right. Our main requirement was that it be an old stone house on the edge of a small village. As the two weeks came to a close, we were becoming increasingly discouraged, as was our agent.

"Madame, you are wasting your time and mine," he said. "I will show you two more places, then I think you must look elsewhere. I am sure you will like both, but I must warn you, they exceed your budget." He showed us a small abandoned hamlet. The entire place was for sale. It was isolated, but quite wonderful. The second property was a seven-bedroom house with an attached barn, two other buildings, two basements, and a large courtyard. It took up a sixth of a small village called Olmet and was known locally as *Chateau d'Olmet*. Perched on a high hill, it featured incredible views. Dale and I immediately decided that this would be our summer home. Little did we ever imagine that we would spend our next 40 summers there.

As promised, the property was over our budget. But we were hooked. The decision to own it was beyond our control. We said yes, and then went looking for an additional $20,000.

When we arrived, the village had only seven full-time residents. Four of the houses in the village were rubble, and an equal number were vacation homes. Today, the summer population explodes to 20 people and all the houses have been rebuilt. Properties were very inexpensive at the time for one simple reason: Olmet was a dry village. The residents depended completely on collecting rainwater.

There was a cistern under the chapel that filled with rainwater running off the chapel roof during the winter. It was used by houses without their own cisterns. Most of the inhabitable houses had their own water storage systems. If the winter was dry, water had to be obtained from a river about two kilometers away. There was no telephone service. Madame Dubisson, one of the residents, ran an illegal line to her house and charged the summer residents for its bill. She went crazy trying to calculate her fee every time we called Lebanon or Saudi Arabia and the United Arab Emirates, the United States, or wherever.

According to a French archaeological study, the foundation of our chapel contained a stone dating from 984 AD. Our house was built on a foundation believed to be from the 1100s, though the house itself was built only in the early 1700s. At its peak, the village had some 30 residents.

Our children and their friends would join us, too, until they grew to an age that meant we could no longer dictate summer schedules. Our son, Adam, invited 14 friends during the summer of 2009 and again in 2011. Our daughter invited 10 of her friends to come to Olmet in 2012. During these periods, we preferred to vacate the premises.

The rules of the house when the kids were young were pretty simple: People could stay up all night if they wanted, but they had to be at the lunch and dinner tables. Two hours of work were required in the afternoons until they reached university age. And there was to be no sleeping with members of the opposite sex under our roof. Our daughter once complained that the rule was nonsensical. "You mean I can sleep with my boyfriend in the barn or the courtyard, but not in the house? That doesn't make sense." She was very bright and much better educated than I and there was only one possible response. I agreed that the rule could not necessarily be justified, but it was a rule nonetheless. Did they obey? We couldn't tell. The place was too big to know what was going on in every single room.

About 15 years ago, an English resident and his wife started a jazz club in a cave underneath their house in the village next to ours. Dale, a jazz aficionado, enjoyed their fortnightly sessions. A few years after its successful launch, the people who started the project, Jennifer and Allen Peele, decided to sell their property. That meant breaking up the band unless another venue could be found. Dale immediately said, "We have a big empty barn. Come take a look. You could use it with no problems." Dale was very enthusiastic; I was only lukewarm. She only saw the fun of the project while I knew it would be a lot of work. But I also knew that against the consortium of Jennifer, Allen, Dale, and the head of the band, Rory, I didn't stand a chance.

We needed to lay down a concrete floor and build a stage and a dance floor. Since we were going to have more than 30 people in there at one time, the law required us to install a toilet and wash basin. New windows had to be installed. Lighting had to be installed, the roof needed to be repaired, a bar had to be constructed, tables and chairs for 70 people had to be purchased, an under-bar refrigerator and a second storage refrigerator needed to be installed, signs had to be made, and local posters had to be arranged every two weeks. Liability insurance needed to be arranged. A small problem with the musicians' union had to be dealt with. Thank goodness we had restored the roof 20 years earlier.

Whether I liked it or not, we now had a jazz club with fortnightly sessions. Dale's job was to help Jennifer collect the money. But Dale so enjoyed chatting with the guests that she became the grand dame and hostess. My job was to finance the project and, once it was up and running, be a gofer for Allen as he tended the bar. "David, we'll need a few more chairs. Can you get some from the house?" and "David, I'm running low on white wine. Get some from one of the refrigerators in the other barn" Or "See whose car is blocking Mr. Giro's car" and sometimes even "David, we might need the petty cash topped up because we may be a little short to pay the band."

Between 40 and 75 people would show up to listen to the jazz. Visitors were always surprised by how quiet people were during the sessions. During the intermission, people would sit or stand around the courtyard and pool. Not once did anyone get thrown out or misbehave in any way. I was astonished at what a smooth operation it was. Allen ran an excellent bar and provided discipline for the band. Jazz artists can be unreliable sometimes.

After seven years, and pretending I was Humphrey Bogart in *Casablanca* — although Ingrid Bergman never showed up — I decided it was time to close.

Although Olmet was a focal point in our lives and for our children, it was never home. As our son, Tony, said, "Home was wherever we were at the time." Dale and I now spend six months of the year there, but the children (now aged 44 - 54) come only when they can. They have their own lives and families. Adam married a South African woman and they have built a retirement home just south of Durban, South Africa. Cece and her partner, who have a house in Ithaca, New York, agreed that there were other places in the world where they wanted to holiday besides Olmet. Tony lives in Vermont and spends most of the winter there in a T-shirt. "It's too hot in Olmet," he says. Our youngest, Eliza, lives seven kilometers away. She and her husband have built their own house outside Lodève, our nearby market town.

French laws regarding inheritance are diabolically complicated and, in our case, unfair to the family. Only one of our four children is related to me by blood. That means that Eliza is entitled to receive half the house. In addition, she gets a share of the remaining half, which is to be divided between the four. Eliza can create a document stating that she wants the property to be divided among the four equally, but it would have no legal basis. She must receive her share and only then can the children do what they wish. But none of them have any interest in owning the house. "Do not die before you sell Olmet" is the common thought. Sometime in the coming five years, we will have to act — hopefully before it's too late. Growing old means letting go of the things you love.

After being at the hospital for seven years, we decided to renew our contract a third time in December 1974. Nevertheless, in spite of this being my last go-around, I was beginning to feel unfulfilled with my work. I started to look objectively at myself and the family situation. We lived in an enviable and privileged position within the community. We had a lovely, large apartment; two full-time servants; and easy access to other services. Our four children were attending excellent local private schools. All our healthcare needs were met by the hospital. On the surface, I had it made. We had a wonderful social life with an incredibly wide circle of friends and colleagues. The political situation may have been a concern, but we learned to live with it.

An economic boom was taking place all around us and I felt left out. I was ready to leave the secure environment of the nonprofit world to join the rough-and-tumble world of the profit-making private sector. It was time to leave the cocoon of university life. But we both wanted to organize our lives in a way that allowed us to remain in Lebanon.

Dale had started her own company, designing and producing woven, modern tapestries or wall hangings. She used Arab motifs as designs in her tapestries, keeping in mind the cultural sensitivities of her clients in the Middle East. With the burst of new office blocks, large private homes, hotels, and corporate offices, there were miles of empty wall space. Based on her art training in Florence and her interest in and understanding of the history and culture of the region, she was confident that she could fill a gap in the commercial art market.

She had nine full-time weavers in two villages outside Beirut and travelled regularly to Damascus, selecting and dyeing wool to her own specifications. Her work was exhibited in cities throughout the Middle East, Europe, and in parts of the United States. The business was a great success. Her client list included not only local people and the expatriate community in Beirut, but the large European and American expatriate communities throughout the Middle East, as well.

Along with her friend Pen Nelson (the wife of Courtney Nelson, head of Ford Foundation projects in the Middle East and Africa), Dale was instrumental in working with the American Women's Club to start a crafts' center. While in Africa, Pen created a company that used local textiles with her contemporary designs. Together, Dale and Pen were very important contributors to the newly established American Women's Club of Beirut Craft Center. Lebanese men and women made various craft objects based on designs created by Pen and Dale. It was designed to appeal to the Western tastes of the time. The Center was such a roaring success that it required larger premises soon after it opened. Dale became a mover and shaker and a bit of a celebrity in the Middle East art scene. She was able to fulfill her role as a professional woman, a mother of four, and a great wife all at the same time.

I did not want her success to be in any way interrupted by my professional ambitions. But I had gone as far as I could. Further promotions in the university hierarchy without a medical degree or a PhD would be impossible.

I had a long discussion with the Dean about my situation and the fact that I was seriously considering leaving the university. He said he would personally prefer that I remained. "But given your interest in the area and where you are at the university, I understand. If I were your age, I would do the same," he said. My job was secure while I looked for another position, so long as I promised to give him three months' notice.

"Just one thing, David," he added. "I'm sure you're aware of the current political situation in Lebanon. Whatever you decide to do, keep this in mind." Truer words were never spoken. He was more perceptive than I thought.

I spoke to Dr. Tabara. He, too, was genuinely sorry to hear about my plan, but he was also sympathetic. Like the Dean, he expressed concern over the political situation. "I wouldn't let that spoil your plans," he said. "After all, you carry a green passport (that was the color of a USA passport back then). That's your safety valve should you need one."

Escape from Beirut

Within two months, I accepted a position with an American company, Charter Medical, based in Macon, Georgia. They wanted to set up an office in the Middle East and asked if I would be interested. They had successfully completed negotiations with an Iranian doctor to staff and manage a 100-bed hospital on Elizabeth Avenue, a smart part of Tehran. My job was to represent the company throughout the Middle East and identify new opportunities.

I was interviewed by the vice president, Robert Crosby ("Call me Bob."), who was the reason I joined the company. I was impressed by his attitude and the manner in which he presented himself. He admitted that he knew nothing about the Middle East and did not have any particular interest in the area except that, "It seems like a place where my company can make some money."

He acted dumb like a fox: "I can teach you something about our company, but I ain't gonna teach you anything about the Middle East. You're gonna teach us," he said. He was generous, good-natured, honest (as far as I could tell), and had a polite, Southern manner. He also had an incredibly uncanny business sense.

Shortly after setting up a small office with a secretary in Beirut, I received a phone call from Bob Crosby. "Could you get on over to *Tear-ron* to hold down the fort? The hospital administrator we employed can't take it anymore and told me he's leavin' on Thursday."

I would spend the next six months in Tehran, only going back to my family and our newly-established office in Beirut for a brief visit every second week. I hit the ground running. Again, I had a feeling that I was out of my depth with no one else to help me this time. After running an established facility with a 100-year history, I walked into a newly-built hospital. It was fully furnished, but I was the only person there. On top of that, Charter Medical, which was supposed to offer support with unlimited funds, had very limited human resources at that time.

The Shah of Iran was becoming increasingly unpopular, and the political ground was shifting. We took no notice of it. That's how naïve we were: wet behind the ears. But with "Call me Bob" and the company's help, we were able to get the hospital staffed and operational within six months. The project proved to be more work than the company anticipated and costs worryingly exceeded the budget. The chief financial officer made his first visit to *Tear-ron* and I could see immediately that he was concerned with not only the financial aspects of the deal, but also the difficulties of supporting such a venture. He did not like Tehran and was no longer impressed with the owner or the medical staff. He made a second trip and left even more discouraged about the project and the increasing uncertainty as to the Shah's ability to rule the country. On his return trip to America, he died of a heart attack on the aeroplane to Atlanta. The project was abandoned.

At the same time, the situation in Beirut was becoming more and more volatile. During the winter and early spring of 1975, minor clashes were building towards an all-out civil war. One of the worst occurred while we were savoring martinis on our balcony as the Lebanese Air Force dive-bombed a Palestinian refugee camp on the outskirts of Beirut.

Then, on the 13th of April, 1975, "an unidentified gunman" in a speeding car fired at the church in the eastern Beirut suburb of Ein El Rumaneh, killing four people, including two Maronite Phalangists. Hours later the Phalangists, led by Bachir Gemayel's militia, killed 30 Palestinians on a bus. This event is considered by most as the start of the Lebanese Civil War. It would go on for another 15 years.

I was still spending most of my time in Tehran. One evening, I got a call from Dale. She told me that the situation in Beirut was particularly bad. The American Embassy had arranged a special flight for all Americans wishing to leave. They were to assemble on the playing field at the American University of Beirut and would be escorted to the airport by the embassy Marine guards and the Lebanese army. We were encouraged to evacuate to Cyprus. But a few of us, including Dale and me, decided to wait out the situation a little longer.

By November, things had continued to deteriorate. It was becoming problematic to fly in and out of Beirut. To create a secure base outside of west Beirut, Arafat had started to set up his Palestine Liberation Organization within the state of Lebanon. The Lebanese authorities were being pushed irrevocably.

I remember very well that second phone call from Dale. She had crawled on the floor of our apartment to get to the telephone and call me. "Hold on and I'll put the receiver up to the window," she said. I could hear the gunfire and bombs. Our Italian friend, Tony Yuja, had said he could arrange for Dale and the children to get on an Alitalia flight that was evacuating the employees of the Italian Embassy. She asked if I could get back to help her before the flight left. It was leaving in five days.

Our sons, Adam and Tony, were going to Brummana, an excellent Quaker school in a small mountain village located about an hour and a half from Beirut. (Incidentally, one of Osama Bin Laden's sons was Tony's classmate.) Dale had to get the boys down from the mountains to our apartment. She needed a Christian driver to take her as far as the Green Line, which separated the Christian and Muslim parts of Beirut. There, she would change cars and a Muslim driver would take her the rest of the way. The same procedure had to be repeated on the way back. The crossing was manned by short-tempered militiamen, both Christian and Shi'a Muslim. There were also Druze and Sunni militia as well as nonreligious groups, which included the Syrian Socialist Nationalist Party and two competing Ba'ath Party factions. Then there were pro-Israeli factions headed by Abdul Majeed Rifaei, a Sunni. All of them were armed and dangerous.

Despite having travelled previously through much of the Middle East and experienced flare-ups, Dale was petrified. The thought of crossing the Green Line alone was too terrifying. But how else would she bring the boys home? Meanwhile, I was trying to get a flight from Iran back to Beirut.

When setting up our representative office in Beirut, I had hired a Druze woman, Leila, who was about 35 and single. The Druze religion started in Lebanon, Israel, and Syria and was an offshoot of the Ismaili sect of Islam. The Druze considered themselves a reformatory sect; you could say they were the Protestants of Islam. Being a Druze, Leila felt confident that she could pass through the two zones safely and fetch the boys. Dale said she should not risk her life for our children. Leila insisted and Dale told me afterwards, "Thank god, she insisted."

Leila said afterward that going up was not so difficult, but there was serious gunfire just before reaching the Green Line on the way back. Tony got on the floor in the back, Adam on the floor in the front, and Leila stretched out on the backseat.

I called Bob Crosby and told him that we were planning to leave, which he fully supported. "Egee," he said, "I don't know how you took it for so long." By the time we left in December 1975, some 600 people had already died in the fighting.

Our family was torn apart when we left Beirut and landed in Rome with 20kg of luggage per person, which was all we were allowed. Writing about it makes me sad to this day, not just because we had to leave Beirut, but also because, having created a wonderful family life and a wonderful professional life, we now had to start all over again. Standing in the Rome airport with no address to go to, no telephone number to call, not a single contact, and with a wife and four children, was daunting.

We headed to the only residence hotel I knew in Rome, *Hotel d'Inghilterra*. I wanted to establish some sense of stability, even if it was only temporary. I refused to envision my family of six living out of suitcases in a hotel, and I wanted to create a whole new lifestyle.

Bob Crosby and I agreed that I would set up temporary accommodations in Rome, renting a place by the month, and using one bedroom as an office. With her usual genius and utter faith in God, Dale found an incredibly nice apartment with a separate entrance to a small, attached office. It was located in Via Della Consulata, a short walk from the Spanish Steps. The first thing we did was to arrange for the kids' schooling. I wanted them in a school that taught in the language they had been instructed in, English or French. The Arabic would have to wait for now. But the urgency with which we left meant we had failed to bring any school records. Thankfully, Leila was able to get a three-line letter confirming that the boys did attend the Brummana School.

We enrolled Eliza, our youngest, in an Italian school run by nuns. It took her about three weeks to learn Italian and she loved the school, her new friends, and the language. The school also had the loveliest Italian mothers, who dropped off and picked up their children twice a day. Dale liked looking at the young Italian fathers and I, the Italian mothers.

Cece, our oldest, had befriended a teacher at her French school in Beirut and she and her husband became our friends in turn. She was able to arrange for Cece to gain admission to an excellent school in Lyon so that she could finish her last two years of the French baccalaureate degree program. She lived with a French family near the school, did exceedingly well, and went on to Harvard University, which would accept her directly into the second year if she chose to do so. Instead, she decided to enter for the entire four years.

I was raised believing that a child must receive the best education possible. But this came at a cost. Cece was banished from her home and family, an exile in a foreign land, living with an unknown family, without a single friend. I always felt guilty about that decision, a feeling that was compounded a few years ago when Cece told me, "I never knew where you were. I never knew where to call home." I often ask myself if it was worth the price.

Our sons, Tony and Adam, were aged 12 and 14. The Brummana School in Lebanon assured us that the Quaker Society would accept the boys into an English Quaker School. Dale, the boys, Eliza, and I went to England to settle the boys into the Friends School in Saffron Walden, Cambridgeshire. It was easier to send the boys away than sending Cece away. I thought then that I had gone away at an equally early age, but what I failed to consider was that I still had a home at the time. In the boys' case, they were leaving everything. Dale and I got teary-eyed when we waved goodbye to them, standing in light, drizzling rain. Eliza sat quietly beside Dale as we drove back to London to return to Rome. Tony settled in and remained at the Friends School for the next three years. When his classmates graduated, with the help of Dale's mother, he got a place at a small college in Johnson, Vermont. Adam, on the other hand, hated the place. He was bullied for being a "Yankee" and felt very out of place. He stayed for only one year and then went to Abu Dhabi with us.

The one who adapted most easily was Eliza. At the time, she was only seven, yet she adjusted to the situation better than any of us. She missed her Beirut friends, but enjoyed her school and new environment. She "worked" in a café at the corner of our street, clearing tables and generally entertaining the family owners.

She soon discovered the opera. The Italian National Opera House in Rome — not one of Italy's best opera houses — was almost next door to our apartment. During the intermission on our first visit, we walked out onto the fire escape. "Oh look!" said Eliza. "Our apartment is right next door." We hadn't realized that our building was separated from the Opera House by only a small alleyway. The next time we went, she started talking to the ushers. It was her habit to talk to strangers. By the end of the performance, Eliza was invited to climb the fire escape during future performances and listen to the opera along with the other ushers. Nine years later, she studied opera at the Manhattanville College in New York City.

And so, in a matter of a few weeks, our family structure had been completely revised. Dale and I firmly believed that this was a temporary situation. In hindsight, my arrangements could have been better; they were predicated on my belief that we would all be back in Beirut in eight months' time. Also misguided was our choice to delay our departure until the last minute rather than coming up with a backup plan when the troubles started. At fault was my hopeless optimism and our commitment to the lifestyle we had created. Leaving the Middle East and returning to America was not an option. We desperately wanted to continue living in the Middle East as a family. Nevertheless, we were grateful to be in the beautiful city of Rome, particularly as Dale had such fond memories of Italy. "We're smoked salmon refugees," she used to say.

We settled into our gypsy lifestyle because we fully intended to go back to Beirut. That was our home. It would be many months before we realized that we could never go back to our penthouse view of the Mediterranean on one side and the city of Beirut on the other. Meanwhile, the situation in Tehran continued to go from bad to worse. Finally, in November 1976, Charter Medical decided to walk away from the Middle East and offered me a choice between a position in Macon, Georgia, or severance pay and resignation. I took the latter.

Up to that point, my whole life had been spent in school or working. This was the first time I was unemployed. It was one of the most desperate times in our married life. I was apprehensive about the future and sad about the recent past. I had a wife and four children and no savings to speak of. Our only tangible asset, at that point, was a broken-down chateau in southwest France, which we had purchased the previous year.

Our children were scattered about at schools in France, Italy, and England.

I was lucky. Two weeks after giving up my job at Charter Medical, I got a call from Bob Crosby, who was now working at Hospital Corporation of America. He invited me to join him and suggested we have a meeting in Nashville. At the meeting, we agreed that I would continue to work out of Rome and if the situation in Beirut did not improve soon, we would set up an office "somewhere in the Middle East."

I was delighted for three reasons. First, I had a new job. Second, HCA was a large and very profitable company with both the resources and staying power to succeed in what became a competitive Middle Eastern market. Finally, they had the experience to appreciate the difficulties in securing new business and maintaining existing projects in the region.

My brief was outlined by Bob Crosby in very simple terms: set up a one-man office with a full-time secretary and a numbers man when I needed one. I was also to identify and evaluate any new hospital management contracts or projects, which could be financed 100 percent by foreign governments. It was also understood that I would act as a trouble-shooter or a stop-gap measure for their projects in Saudi Arabia and anywhere else in the region. The company, which owned or managed 600 hospitals in America and various foreign locations, was able to "finance my total operation out of a petty cash drawer."

Our period in Rome lasted just short of two years. It was probably the most gloomy time we spent together. I travelled extensively — our future was uncertain and Dale could not continue her work. Until then in my career, projects, opportunities, information, and contacts all came to me. As the Director of the American University Hospital, I was sought after. Now my life was totally reversed. I had no training in marketing or sales. I had never worked in "business development." My contacts were those who needed me, but now I had to find contacts I needed. What if I couldn't find any projects? Did I have the natural instinct for sniffing out opportunities? Was I really an entrepreneur? I felt completely alone. I admitted to myself that I really didn't know what the hell I was doing.

When I called Bob Crosby for reassurance, his view, as always, was to "just keep building smoke — we'll get there." He didn't have a business plan; I didn't have a budget to work with or specific objectives to meet.

When I did receive telephone calls from the head office, it was invariably to look after some member of the board or senior executive who happened to be visiting my area of responsibility. Could I look after such and such and "Where is a good place for him to jog? Can you take them out to dinner? Can you suggest a good restaurant?"

It was also the lowest point in Dale's adult life. She had had a thriving and successful business in Beirut with nine full-time weavers producing tapestries. She had works in progress that were never finished. Her stock was sent out of Lebanon and stored in Rome and New York. She tried to keep the momentum going by making trips to Europe and America, but it was unsatisfactory. She soon realized that America and Europe were not interested in her tapestries so she reluctantly closed down the business. Except for our daughter Eliza, she was alone. My responsibility was to be in the Middle East, so I was away a lot. Her life was very empty with no work, three of her four children away from home, and her husband travelling extensively. I felt disheartened for Dale but could do nothing about it. When we were together, we were together full-time. We lived just for one another.

Dubai

As long as it was in the Arab Middle East, Bob had left it up to me to decide where to set up an office. We wanted to feel that we were in the old Arab world and at the same time live without the conservative restrictions of Islam. In other words, an Arab country where we could do as we did in Lebanon, buy alcohol, and avoid places that restricted women from wearing skimpy bathing suits or disallowed them from driving. Dubai seemed to us the most civilized city in the region and by civilized, I mean the most heathen. But it still maintained its ancient Arab trading spirit. As we prepared to leave for Dubai, we knew that we would fly 30,000 feet above Beirut while en route.

At the time, Dubai seemed to still retain some old Arab characteristics, which was particularly true of the life along the creek. The creek is Dubai: it gave the city a shape and a direction. I suppose it was like the Seine in Paris. One went up the creek, down the creek, across the creek, over the creek, on the creek and later, they built a tunnel so you could go under the creek, too. It was vital for both commerce and the residents' lives.

Hence, we were certain about only one aspect of our move to Dubai: We would live on the creek, in the middle of the city. It was the only place in the entire Gulf that remained historical and picturesque, but still livable. We saw a building on the creek with office space and residential accommodations. The location was exactly what we wanted, but there was only one problem. The building was not quite finished. We were assured that it would be ready for occupancy within a few weeks. We hadn't lived in Beirut for nothing. I knew a few weeks meant a few months. We lived up the road at the Intercontinental Hotel for five months.

On looking back, it was the start of a two-year period of underlying despair for Dale and the kids. Not returning to Beirut and the Beirut lifestyle was now a sad reality. Being in Rome had been tolerable for Dale because there was always the hope of going back. But now reality had to be confronted. She had to find something to do besides sunning herself by the hotel swimming pool and waiting for the apartment to be completed.

Finding a school for the children was difficult, as was everything else. At the time, there were no expatriate schools for Western children. The only exception was the French oil company, Total, which had set up a small school for their own employees' children. Dale managed to get Eliza and Adam accepted. It consisted of a collection *port-à-cabins* (used for officers' accommodations at the numerous construction sites around the country). All instruction was in French. Today, the only memory Adam has of this particular experience was the ride back to the hotel and to the school in an un-air-conditioned school bus in blistering 43° centigrade temperatures.

When we finally moved into our new apartment, it was finished in the local sense of the word. The lift was unpredictable (we lived on the seventh floor), the water supply was intermittent, and there was still work going on in the building. Some of the corridors still had pieces of plasterboard and electric cable dangling from the false ceilings. But it was a wonderful large apartment, with the most spectacular view that anyone could want in Dubai.

Over time, we met some friends and were adopted by a small Swedish community involved in shipping contracts. They were all younger than us and looked very attractive at our regular beach outings. Entertainment was thin on the ground: no movies except for old-fashioned videotapes, no television except for Arab speaking Egyptian soap operas, and no cultural events. My greatest small pleasure was to enjoy the bird's-eye view of the creek and its activities from our balcony. Looking to the right, I could see the sun sink into the Gulf. There was an orange afterglow, but no spectacular sunsets.

The local sailing boats, called *dhows*, would be double-parked like the cars down wharf-side. As it got darker, small groups of men would be hunched over charcoal stoves, preparing their dinner on the decks before spreading themselves out to sleep. They worked and they slept in their loose, hand-sewn trousers, threadbare shirts, and simple sandals. During the day, they loaded the *dhows* mostly by hand, except when an old handmade derrick was brought along wharf-side to plop a red Toyota sedan onto the dock. It looked like it hadn't changed in centuries.

Late in the evenings, when all the men were fast asleep, we would walk along the creek, enjoying the cool of the evening and observing the dhow owners in their white robes thumbing their worry beads. Another evening pleasure was hiring a water taxi — essentially a long, narrow boat that was so crowded with commuters in the daytime that everyone had to stand. It cost pennies, but in the evening, when the boats were empty and drivers were half asleep, you could hire one for a ride along the entire creek. It cost a good deal more pennies, but it was worth it.

We would return to dinner prepared by our Indian houseboy, James. Our son, Adam, described James as follows: "Mischievous, creative, optimistic, caring, and often drunk. James would create his daily delicacies by collecting the best ingredients from the souk, carefully prepare them into a full meal, and then serve them with great fanfare while completely hammered."

After being in Dubai for six months, things started to pick up for Dale. While living in Beirut, she had met an important Bahraini sheikh who was part of the ruling family. He was blind and responsible for the education and welfare of blind people in Bahrain. They talked about the possibility of teaching blind people to weave. Dale made contact with him, and he invited her to spend several weeks teaching some blind students to weave.

Also when we lived in Beirut, she had met a wealthy merchant, who lived in Dubai and was building a new shopping mall that included a 300-bed Hyatt Regency Hotel, a conference center, shops, and an ice-skating rink — unique at the time in Dubai. Dale's career as a weaver was about to be rebranded as a Middle Eastern art consultant. Based on her experience in Beirut, she was asked to design and execute tapestries for his hotel, under the direction of his Italian interior designer. Dale and the designer were responsible for the artwork for the entire complex.

The challenge changed her attitude towards Dubai and the loss of Beirut. She took the job of supplying and installing all the artwork for the rooms, public areas, restaurants, offices and the ice-rink (she proposed a life-size copy of an early flying machine suspended over the rink). It was a huge project requiring many hours pouring over architects' drawings and travelling in the Middle East and Europe commissioning massive pieces of art. The project consumed her to the point that she delayed a trip to America to see her critically-ill father and arrived in Vermont only a few hours before he died because she was so busy. Our daughter, Eliza, was convinced that she was having an affair with her boss. She didn't know he was gay.

Libya

I was sitting in my office in Dubai when Bob Crosby called.

"David, do you remember the Libya consulting contract that I told you about?"

"Yeah," I said. He had mentioned it briefly in passing during an earlier phone conversation.

"Well, according to our agent, Mahmoud Chara, it looks like the Ministry of Health is going to sign a contract. I want you to get over to Libya as soon as you can to see what's going on." He added, "I just never thought they'd really sign it." Much later, I understood what he meant.

The corporate executives of HCA had reluctantly considered the deal because a member of the board of directors with an interest in Libya had put gentle pressure on Tommy Frist, the President of HCA, to accept the "opportunity." Besides, they had no one in the company who knew the situation in Libya well enough to object. So, even as they went through the motions, the people on the ground never thought they would be awarded the contract.

The Libyan health ministry wanted to make an agreement with a company to draw up specifications for the medical equipment required for two 800-bed hospitals under construction: one in Tripoli and the other in Benghazi. (It would eventually be 15 years before they became operational.) The Ministry intended to create a tender proposal based on the specifications. We were also required to write up an administrative directive to be used for the operation of the two hospitals and the required staff to run both facilities. The contract was expected to take no more than 18 months, for which HCA would receive $10 million.

I can hear it now: "Come on guys; it's a win-win situation. If we don't win the contract, we don't want it anyway. And if we do win, we've got enough fat in it to do the job and make a hell of a profit."

But in spite of HCA's multimillion-dollar turnover and its huge financial resources, not a single employee had any appreciation of the hostile environment and the difficult working circumstances Libya presented. The corporate personnel in Nashville seemed oblivious to the State Department's human rights report, which accused Libya of making arbitrary arrests and being rabidly anti-Israel. They had no idea that the country was accused of "external aggression; threatening regional peace; exporting its domestic revolution; adapting a revisionist orientation; and systematically violating human rights." All that the company knew and cared about was that it might be awarded $10 million for work they thought could easily be carried out at minimal cost.

I had never been to Libya, never thought seriously about going there, and knew little to nothing about it. But it was I who had to "get over there and see what was going on."

This was 1977. Colonel Gaddafi had taken over from King Idris in September 1969, when he was only 27 years old. On taking power, along with a small group of military officers, Gaddafi immediately closed down the American and British military bases. Shortly thereafter, he nationalized all foreign oil and commercial interests. Most development projects had been awarded to Communist Eastern European countries. There were few technical contracts awarded to Western companies. Ours was a rarity.

I flew to Tripoli and checked into the Libya Palace Hotel in order to meet Mahmoud Chara, our local contact. His was the only name I had in the entire country. It turned out he was in the US, but due back "immediately."

The Libya Palace Hotel overlooked what once was described as the beautiful and romantic bay of Tripoli, a wonderful, old, colonial city with 19th-century Italian architecture. By the time I arrived, however, the city was dirty, unpainted, and falling apart. It was uncared for. The port was packed with millions of shipping containers, seven stories high, and hundreds of ships waiting to be unloaded. It was probably the ugliest bay in North Africa.

Built in late 1930, the hotel itself was a "modern structure." It was being held together by spit and bailing wire. Those of us who were privileged enough to secure a room were grateful, especially if we considered the other options. The privilege, incidentally, was granted based on the size of the bribe you were prepared to pay and was regularly reviewed after a four-day stay. (No one in his or her right mind would want to stay more than four nights anyway). The hotel was occupied mostly by Eastern European company executives. There was no menu. Breakfast was always the same small, buffet-style, Eastern European breakfast with lots of cheese and substitute ham (pork was not allowed). Lunch and dinner were whatever was available on that day, but you could be guaranteed that at dinner, the first course would be a soup left over from the lunch that afternoon. Whatever the main course was, it came from a can or frozen pack, as did the dessert. Two weeks after Esso discovered oil in 1959, the Libyans and their masters — the Italians — got out of the farming business. They decided it was cheaper and easier to import food. Most of it came from Yugoslavia, Bulgaria, Poland, or Romania.

In what was the hotel lounge bar, they sold Eastern European canned fruit juice or club soda mixed with cranberry syrup, which was highly prized because it was the only thing that passed for an alcoholic drink. There was a telex machine in the corner of the lounge, spitting out the events of the day. The hotel's one television showed mostly Egyptian sitcoms,

Libyan news, and cultural programs. The government had taken ownership of the hotel a few years earlier and, like most government-controlled businesses, standards were low.

Mahmoud's immediate return occurred two weeks later. In the meantime, his assistant, Brian Williams, was my only contact. He was unhelpful and never really knew when his boss would return. Poor Brian was one of the few independent Western engineers left in the country. He was not a paper-pusher, but a doer. He'd been knocking around North Africa, working in Egypt, Tunisia, and Libya, for the past 30 years. He suffered from the staying-on syndrome of the early Gaddafi reign. Every time people thought it couldn't get any worse, it did.

When Mahmoud finally came back from the US, he seemed unconcerned about my welfare or state of mind. I would learn that waiting around for weeks was all part of being in Libya. "If you had to live in Libya with a family of four daughters, wouldn't you delay your return for as long as possible?" Mahmoud joked. I had to agree with him. He was a relaxed, warm, and friendly man. I would come to enjoy working with him.

Mahmoud occupied a very nice house, to which he was entitled as a senior executive of the Esso Oil Company prior to nationalization. He could stay there for the rest of his life, but he had lost his job because he was not a relative or friend of the minister of petroleum. He made his living as a contact man or fixer for anyone in need.

Nothing fazed Mahmoud, no matter how bad things got. He was never angry, never felt cheated, and was never envious of others. He had the temperament for survival in Libya. I tried desperately to imitate him and he always reminded me to remain cool. On two occasions, after coming through the Customs hall at Heathrow, he asked me, "How come my bags always get searched and yours don't?" I'm sure he knew the answer, and he seemed to accept it.

The only time I saw Mahmoud surprised was when he discovered that we might actually get the contract. He knew very little about it himself. "I'll need some time to see what's going on," he said. "Meanwhile, why don't you go back to Dubai?"

A few weeks later, we signed a consultancy agreement with the Ministry of Health, which stipulated that a senior company representative be "in country" 30 days after the signing of the contract. Although living in Dubai at the time, I asked to be the acting director while recruiting a permanent one.

I moved to Libya while Dale's work on the hotel, conference center, and shopping mall in Dubai kept her busy back in the Emirates. We carried on our husband and wife relationship as best we could with dirty weekends away in various parts of the world. Our children were scattered around, with one in school in France, one in Vermont and two in Dubai. It was not an easy time, but there was no other way.

A requirement for signing the contract was to obtain a performance bond that was satisfactory to the Libyan government, but not too onerous for HCA. This presented quite a challenge, particularly as there were limited diplomatic relations between the US and Libya, and all foreign banks had been taken over by the government. There was only one bank in the country and that belonged to Gaddafi. However, we eventually managed after nearly two months, and only because HCA was a very good client of Bank of America in New York. The next task was to secure our first prepayment. I would personally go to the Libyan National Bank nearly every day for about two months. I quickly learned that we would not receive any payments without first establishing personal contacts at every level in the bank.

Mahmoud seemed reluctant to go with me, so he coached me from the sidelines. This task was aided by bringing chocolates for various clerks from my regular trips to London and Dubai. The clerks were often female and usually wives of Egyptian and Tunisian contract workers in Libya. They lived modestly, sending most of their pay back to their families in their home countries. I also brought back the latest calculators or any other portable gadgets that I thought the male clerks might want.

The Libyans who took over the jobs of the Western banking personnel would spend most of their day drinking tea or coffee, provided by elderly Egyptian tea-boys. I could never figure out what exactly Libyan government servants did. They would sit at their desks behind stacks of papers. Whenever I needed to see them, they were either on the phone, in meetings, or travelling abroad, generally to Communist countries. The current hot spot was North Korea. It seemed that every Libyan bank employee had been on a government-sponsored conference to North Korea, was going on one, or hoped to go on one. Apparently, Bulgaria and Yugoslavia were "old hat."

I finally got word that Bank of America received our first prepayment, which was deposited into the Libyan National Bank in Tripoli. It was all in cash. They had a wonderful way of counting bank notes, which was the only other thing Libyan bank employees did. A stack of notes was folded between the little finger and the forefinger, with the thumb pushing each bill to one side and counting as they went along. This was incredibly fast and surprisingly accurate.

All my transactions for the projects were carried out in cash, including renting offices, paying salaries, purchasing cars, and paying bribes. In Tripoli, I was able to rent an attractive office in the center of town, next to the arched entrance of the old *medina* previously owned by a foreign company. A close friend of Mahmoud's had "acquired" it. That it had telephone and telex lines was a real surprise. Colleagues and friends could not believe it. The rent and the administration fee were paid in cash every quarter.

The office came with a part-time secretary — a fat, lazy, Libyan woman who presented me with a shopping list every time I took a trip out of the country. But we got along. She knew a lot of people and was an effective gofer who was happy for any excuse to get out of the office. She introduced me to an accountant, Boulos, who was polite and well-mannered, and insisted on calling me "Mr. Egee." He worked for a Libyan company in the morning and for me in the late afternoon. Most of his earnings were sent back to his wife and family in Egypt. When I tried to get a reference on him, I found that no Libyan would give an Egyptian a good reference. The Libyans resented the fact that they had to depend on Egyptians. In turn, the Egyptians resented the fact that they had to find work in Libya. Boulos kept telling me how you could never trust Libyans, when at the same time the Libyans always told me how you could never trust Egyptians.

I hired Boulos strictly on faith. He appeared intelligent and honest. I had no way of quizzing his accountancy abilities or any way of measuring his skills, except by verifying that he could add and subtract correctly. We would sit together every week so he could show me exactly what monies we were spending and what had been transferred back to the head office. He was an accountant, office manager, and fixer. He knew how to get anything and everything done through friends or friends of friends.

Having a telephone line in Libya was a big deal, but to be able to make calls outside of Libya was something else altogether. It seemed that only Libyans were permitted to work as telephone operators because, once again, they were the only ones the government could trust. Boulos just happened to know one. "I'll have him come by the office tomorrow after five," he said.

At ten minutes past five, Ashraf appeared. He said he would phone my office every day that he was on duty, between five and ten past five. He would simply ask, "How can I help you?" I would give him the location and telephone number. It was quite amazing. I could hear him speaking to operators all over the world. "Hello, Chicago, this is Libya calling. Can you connect me with London, please?"

"One moment, sir."

I would come on the line.

"Hello, may I help you?" London would ask.

"Yes, this is Libya calling, can you connect me with Nashville 555-5555?" That party would answer and I could hear Ashraf saying, "I have a call for you from Libya. Hold on, please." He would come on the line to me, saying, "Okay, David, I have your party." At the end of the call, after I put down the receiver, he would call me right back. "Do you need another call, David?"

Once a month, Boulos paid Ashraf $100 and entered "phone charges" into the accounts' book. We never received a proper invoice from the Libyan telephone company, if there even was such a thing.

A few months into the contract, Hans Season, the Finance Director for HCA Europe, sent me a telex saying he would be visiting Libya "to review the accounts." I was anxious about his visit, but Boulos was in a state of complete panic. To him, there was only one reason someone from the finance department of the head office would travel all the way from Nashville to Libya: because there was a problem, and the problem would be his fault.

Hans was a no-nonsense person who spoke with lots of pauses. He was suspicious of nearly everyone and was certain that everyone was "trying to fuck the accounting department." Hans said to me afterwards that he had been told to come to Libya to find out "what the hell Egee is doing over there." Then he added, "Egee, do you want to know something?"

There was a long pause.

"I came out here expecting to find a real mess. I came ready to close you out."

Another long pause.

"Why?" I asked, nervously.

"Well, for a start, I checked what you were being paid to sit over here and get this job started, and you know what I found?"

Pause.

"I found you haven't cashed a paycheck for the past four months, so I figure you gotta be cheating. I mean, how you gonna live? Then I find out that you hired this goddamn Egyptian to track the finances of this office."

Pause.

"Running a ten million dollar consultancy contract, all in cash!"

Longer pause.

"Buying two cars out of expenses! Ain't nobody in Nashville who knows anything about this contract. And if you ask me, they don't wanna know about it."

Yet another pause.

"So, Egee, I figured it's a situation with a lot of shenanigans."

An even longer pause.

"But I'll tell you something, Egee; I can't find anything wrong. It looks like all the cash has been accounted for, and I really can't find anything for the head office to justify me kicking your ass. You're running this damn place the only way you can." Pause. "I guess."

I breathed as he paused yet again. In a low voice he said, "Besides, who the hell else are they going to get to come over to this godforsaken country with a madman running it? After that trip to the National Bank of Libya, and after what I see here, Egee, you're not going to get anyone from Nashville to come out here on a permanent basis. If you can get that goddamn Egyptian a Green Card, I'd hire him to work in my department."

And with that, Hans went back to America, leaving Boulos very pleased with himself. He had been offered a job in America, and I was secure in my position because no one else wanted it.

Since 1970, there had been a steady deterioration of American and Libyan relations, which led, in 1972, to the American government closing its embassy and downgrading the status of the ambassador's position to that of *chargé de affaires*.

In 1977, when I arrived in Tripoli, Bill Eagleton, the then *chargé d'affaires*, contacted me at my hotel. He invited me to his office, where I met Brooks Buxton, the government relations officer for the CONOCO oil company. He was interested in my presence in Tripoli only because I was, to his knowledge, among very few American businessmen living in Tripoli at that time. There were other Americans in the country, but they were involved in oil production and remained incarcerated in their compounds in the middle of the desert. I would see these Americans on the British Caledonia flight coming into and leaving Libya. They would drink huge quantities of beer on their departure from Libya, having been without it for long periods of time. One time, a flight attendant took pity on Dale just 20 minutes into the flight and moved her to the first class section to escape their behavior.

Brooks Buxton seemed like a "waspy," East Coast-type of person, as was Bill Eagleton. Both were Arab experts and had a fluent knowledge of Arabic. They were also extremely intelligent and well-educated, as was Bill Eagleton's wife. Brooks was single. I assumed Brooks was CIA and the CONOCO employee story was only a cover-up. Eagleton had a great interest in tapestries and Oriental carpets and was therefore interested to know what Dale was doing in the field of textiles. For Dale and me, they were a breath of fresh air in this cultural and intellectual wasteland.

There was another American working and living in Tripoli, Ed Wilson, but he was quite another story. He would fill a number of columns and inches of newsprint with his activities in Libya five years later when he was arrested. On my first trip to Libya, he was seated next to me in the first class section of a British Caledonia flight. Ed was an extremely gregarious man who flattered people by seeming genuinely interested in the person with whom he was talking. He asked intelligent questions about my work, family, and interests; and gave just enough of himself away to make me interested in him. At the end of the day, he had learned much more about me than I had about him. I told him I worked for HCA.

"Really! Do you know of a chap, Cal Pastors?"

"Yes." I said. "In fact, Cal told me to look you up while in Tripoli if I had the chance. He said that you were a real character and you worked together on some projects in the CIA."

"Did he mention which ones?"

"Well," I replied, "he told me about Cuba, Vietnam, and about digging up gold coins from World War Two."

He laughed and talked about the same stories Cal had told me. I can't say we became good friends, but we certainly became acquaintances and occasionally visited each other's offices. He told me quite frankly that he worked for the CIA and was providing medical equipment to the health authority and the military and was also providing training for military medics. His office was a large second-floor open space with two private interview rooms and a group of six tables off in one corner, and several metal bookshelves, stacked from floor to ceiling with medical equipment catalogues, which seemed to be placed on any flat surface available.

Ed introduced me to six military medics who had just come from four months of training in the desert and were on rotation back to America. I was struck by the fact that they were all muscular and of medium height, and probably worked-out a lot. Rather than the tall, skinny, slightly undernourished male nurses I generally saw, they were stereotypical physical education instructors.

There were six telephones in the place, one on every desktop. Our conversations were constantly interrupted by Ed taking calls on different phones. He would talk in a low voice, standing beside one of the desks with his back turned to his visitor. Otherwise, he would speak very loudly, which was fine by me because I was starting to go deaf at the time. He never walked between the desks, but rushed as if hurrying to rescue a boiling pot on a hot stove. Ed had an attractive Mediterranean assistant, but she never answered any of the phones. Ed seemed to be the only one allowed to take calls. No wonder he was in such good shape.

He once asked if I could help him purchase, through our HCA supply system, two shipping containers of disposable nappies from Kimberly Clarke. With 600 private hospitals, we were a major client of Kimberly Clarke's medical supply division, so I didn't think it would be a problem. John Trescott, who was the head of the HCA international supply department made some inquiries on my behalf and got back to me.

"No way would Kimberly Clarke be able to supply such a large order on such short notice," John said. "And they were very suspicious of such a large order being placed by an unknown but infamous source."

I told Ed the order was too big for HCA to handle. I didn't want to ask what he intended to do with the disposable nappies. Battlefield dressings just didn't add up. Another time, he asked if I could arrange a venue in one of our hospitals for him to put on a three-day conference near his home in Virginia. It would be for 20 military doctors. He would arrange their transportation and accommodations. We just needed to provide the venue and the lectures. He added that there would be a very nice fee involved for HCA.

I called Bob Crosby, who was by now the president of HCA International. I could tell from his voice that he was less than enthusiastic. I told him that it was probably just an excuse to arrange a holiday trip for officers in the military, but it needed to be wrapped around a plausible event. We discussed it, and I told Ed that HCA could not do it because the higher echelons thought it might be too controversial. He accepted this without question.

Ed was such an enthusiastic individual. He had a wide range of interests. He was knowledgeable about cultural events and had a particular interest in Arab history, archaeology, and artifacts. We visited Leptis Magna, Sabratha, and Cyrenaica together. It was really quite marvelous to approach these ancient sites without another living soul in the area. There were no fences, no "visitors' parking" signs, no snack bars — just these isolated, untouched monuments. I enjoyed his company; helped no doubt by his inexhaustible supply of whisky, beer, and wine in a country where possession of such items meant 40 lashes just for starters.

Some years later, I was saddened to read, "On February 5, 1983, the Houston, Texas, Federal Court tried the former CIA Agent, Edwin P. Wilson, on federal charges of unlawfully selling 42,000 pounds (20 tons) of the plastic explosive C4 to Libyan Dictator, Muammar Gaddafi. Wilson hired former Green Berets to work in an institutional training program to train people in the use of such materials. He was convicted and sent to prison to serve 52 years in solitary confinement. The CIA stated that Ed Wilson had not worked for them since 1972."

You mean to tell me that Ed Wilson and six ex-Green Berets stole 42,000 pounds of the most lethal explosives manufactured in that day, and the CIA had nothing to do with it?

Meanwhile, trying to start and manage the project was becoming increasingly difficult. The fault lay partly with me. I had no experience setting up a multimillion-dollar consultancy engineering project. But the fault lay partly with the company, too. They did not have the expertise or an appreciation of working conditions. Nor did they have anyone within the organization willing to travel to Libya. And the fault lay partly with the Libyan Government.

Bob Crosby was sympathetic to my situation, but he was having difficulty identifying qualified people to take part in the project. I remember Bob's words well: "Egee, just do the best you can. Just keep making smoke and we'll get some people right out there, you hear?"

"Yeah, I hear you," I said.

A few days later, I received a call from Bob's assistant, Dick. "Egee, we've got you a good man — the best — and he's coming out. He'll be there in ten days. His name is Geoff Conner, the godfather of hospital equipment."

Surprised that I hadn't been called to at least discuss a candidate, I asked where he had last worked.

"He worked for Whittaker, in Saudi Arabia, so he knows the environment and he is highly qualified. He'll be a good man."

I remembered Paul Dingle, a senior executive in the Whittaker Corporation, from my American University Hospital days. Since he was responsible for all their Middle Eastern development work, I called him.

"Yeah, I know him," he said. "We had him for a job in Riyadh, Saudi Arabia. I didn't know him personally but I do know that we had to send him back home. He didn't work out, but I don't know the reasons. Why do you want to know?"

"He's coming to work for me in Libya," I said.

"What the hell are you doing in Libya?"

I admitted that I really didn't know myself and cut the conversation short. I was furious. I called Dick back and told him what I had learned.

"Well, Egee, that was the only man we could find," he said. Now it was my problem.

Geoff arrived and reviewed the little paperwork that existed. After a careful look at the contract and our responsibilities, and after a visit to one of the 800-bed hospitals, he said, "No way can we do this job alone." He rattled off a list of experts we were going to need, which included at least four equipment specialists and four technicians. Job descriptions for each position needed to be outlined and a paper had to be prepared showing exactly how we were going to implement and execute the project.

He then went on, at length, about the importance of learning from the client what they expected, what their requirements were, and what their needs would be. We couldn't do anything without in-depth meetings with the client. I suddenly remembered that this was the way consultants worked. They would talk to the client, getting them to tell the consultant what they wanted and how they wanted it done. The consultant would then write up a big report saying what the client had told them. In this case, Geoff would not accept that the client had no idea what he wanted, what he needed, or how he wanted it done.

Our client, the Assistant Minister of Health, was a trained civil engineer. More importantly, he was also a senior member of the People's Committee for Health Workers (unions were forbidden). I told Geoff that the Assistant Minister expected us to tell him what he needed even though he wasn't interested in talking with us in the first place. All he wanted, on his desk, in four months' time, was a preliminary equipment list. He would look at it, find two or three things wrong, give it back to us, and tell us to come back in four weeks. All the client really wanted to know was what percentage he could realistically expect to get for awarding the contract.

Geoff Conner and I flew back to Austin, Texas, where the head office for HCA's supply department was located. We agreed that Jim Steward would be responsible for assembling our preliminary equipment list by using the inventory of our largest 400-bed hospital and doubling it. He intended to ask the supplier to provide updated specifications, which would be attached as part of the report. As Crosby said, "Just keep making smoke." In the meantime, we received regular payments from the Libyan government.

The night before it was time for us to return to Libya, Geoff called me. "My doctor said I should not return to Libya," he said. "He will be sending me a written report. Do you want a copy?" I told him it would not be necessary, and I never saw him again.

By 1977, it was getting more and more difficult to carry out daily activities. One example occurred when the country ran out of salt. It started in the hotel. Suddenly, the saltshakers disappeared. There was no salt in stores throughout Tripoli. We had to drive halfway to Benghazi before we found a shop willing to sell us salt, and that was only because the owner took pity on Dale. He handed her a small bag of carefully wrapped salt from a shelf under the cash register. What safer place to keep such a valuable item?

My unease increased when the "Green Book" was published and widely distributed. It was a tribute to Mao Tse Tung's "Red Book." Every single person in Libya received a copy. It was literally a green book, three volumes long, outlining an alternative method of government and an alternative to Communism and Capitalism. It was a new government system called *Jamahiriya*, which meant "state of the masses." All legal codes would be based on this new system in which power was held by the people through various committees called People's Revolutionary Committees. Sharia law would now relate only to matters of religion. It was the Declaration of the Establishment of the Authority of the People, and it was to be implemented immediately.

According to a report from the US Department of State, Undersecretary for Democracy and Global Affairs, the consequences were "confusion, corruption, lack of transparency, and arbitrary arrests for the domestic population. The government would no longer protect the rights of foreign workers [such as me], migrants, asylum seekers, or refugees." The report went on to say, "Establishing the revolutionary committees would herald the start of institutional chaos, economic decline and general arbitrariness."

The People's Revolutionary Committee took control of all small industries and companies: restaurants, stores, petrol stations, and small shops. Wherever there was a policeman, there was a member of the People's Revolutionary Committee for law enforcement standing right beside him, wearing a newly distributed People's Police armband. Schools were infected by members of the People's Revolutionary Committee for Teachers. I could not comprehend how *Jamahiriya* was going to function; even Mahmoud couldn't explain it to me.

Anti-American feelings began to deepen. When the Egyptian president Anwar Sadat received $12 billion in US military aid after Abdul Nasser's death, Gaddafi saw it as a threat. He broke off relations with Egypt when Sadat visited Israel in 1977. This distrust of Egypt's new government spilled over into distrust of the numerous Egyptians who carried out all of the functions of the civil service throughout Libya. Gaddafi resented the fact that passports were written in English and required all foreigners entering the country to have passports translated into Arabic.

The Carter Administration in the US started to view Libya's activities as no longer relatively innocuous "Muslim solidarity." They were labeled terrorist activities. Despite his distrust of Socialism, Gaddafi turned increasingly towards the Soviet Union for military and industrial aid. In America, Gaddafi was referred to as a fanatic and terrorist. But still, the oil flowed from Libya, providing heat and electricity to New York, New Jersey, and Connecticut, where my parents still lived.

I was feeling increasingly isolated. Dale had long ago made it clear that she would come to Libya only for visits. The more she learned about Libya, the more ill at ease she became. In the meantime, we met in Dubai, London, or Athens. In the evenings, I would walk along the port of Tripoli, catching glimpses of the old city as it had been under during the Italian occupation. I would have dinner in the homes of friends and acquaintances or read books that I was able to bring with me from my trips to London. I kept a diary. It was a lonely life. The saddest moments were taking visiting HCA consultants back to the airport for their return to Europe and America. I knew I had to see the assignment through to the end. I felt like I had been sent to the Army for two years. I needed to provide for my wife and four children. I felt they deserved a lifestyle as good as the one I had while growing up, with all the advantages of a good, private education.

I wanted to remain in the healthcare business on an international level and I had nearly 12 years' experience in the field. Like it or not, it was the only product I had to sell, and I was working with the best of only three American companies that valued my skills. My instincts told me that if I stuck it out as long as possible, things would work out. I believed that if I performed for the company, they would return the gesture.

In early December 1977, there was a huge demonstration in Tripoli as part of the burning of the US Embassy. Like all demonstrations in Tripoli, people seemed to come out of nowhere. There was no announcement and nothing in the papers. I had not heard anything about it from my connections; but suddenly, there it was.

It started in a park, near the old king's palace, now called People's Hall. The crowd headed towards Green Square, near the port. I happened to be out on the street, but not near the demonstration itself. Suddenly a mob of young men appeared. They were walking fast and excitedly towards the square. I was far ahead of them, but I started to feel threatened. I was obviously a foreigner and they could most likely tell I was American. I could feel myself getting tense. They may not have been interested in me at all but, at that moment, I wanted to be safely away.

They started to shout louder. I thought I might have caught their attention. I quickly turned into the next street, ran for a short distance, and then turned into another street and waited. As they seemed to be continuing towards the square, I continued on home.

It turned out that the crowd stormed the US Embassy. Robert D. Kaplan wrote about Eagleton's experience during the attack in Foreign Affairs: "We had a plan on how to get into the secure area — through a secret passage to some adjoining apartments. I ordered the staff to shred and burn all sensitive materials."

The mob stormed the embassy as a response to Carter's attempt to rescue the American diplomats being held in the American Embassy in Tehran.

I was not surprised to get a telex message from Terry Smith the following afternoon. He wanted me to go to London immediately in order to attend "an important meeting." I knew what he was concerned about, but I did not want to do anything immediately. I think I got some secret joy from their concerns. I waited for his second message. He explained that, in light of the current situation, the company did not want to be responsible for anything that might happen to me. He wanted me out of the country as soon as possible. In spite of my assurances to the contrary, people in Nashville, with limited international experience, imagined the worst for me. Terry wasn't going to be persuaded, and I was secretly happy to leave. I was the only employee in Libya at that moment, except for our agent, Mahmoud, and our trusted accountant, Boulos, and I had to trust them to say nothing.

Today, I can't really remember the details and I can't really believe that it all happened. It was as if I was moving in a dream, mechanically. I went to my usual travel agent and purchased a round-trip ticket to London. I went to my house and put a few things into a carry-on bag. I drove my brand new Fiat estate wagon to the airport car park and left the keys on the floor of the car. I walked into the departure lounge, to the check-in counter, through Customs, and left Libya.

I never went back. I never saw or heard from Mahmoud or Boulos again. Oddly, HCA continued to receive regular payments in our bank account for months afterwards.

England

So many good things in my professional career seem to have happened by chance. Some days, God would just smile down on me.

At the same time I left Libya in December 1977, HCA decided to start a chain of private hospitals in England. This venture was to be funded by the profits being made from the King Faisal Hospital project in Saudi Arabia, which were languishing in the Cayman Islands. Rather than bring the money into America, it would be reinvested in an environment in which it was easier to do business.

Offices were established in London, and I was asked to be the director of development. The corporate team was headed by the president of HCA Europe and the Middle East. In addition, there was a lawyer, a finance director, a systems engineer, and an operations director. None of us knew very much about the private healthcare business in England. There was no feasibility study or formal business plan for the six of us to work from. The funds were available, so we took a gamble.

But all of these Americans would need to be housed and fed. We were living in one of the world's most expensive cities. We would have huge start-up expenses. It was my responsibility to find something to justify the extraordinary financial commitment as soon as possible.

Living in countries where I didn't know the language, I had lost interest in watching television. But in London one evening, I caught a glimpse of an interview on the BBC. They were talking to a man who had started three private hospitals. The following morning, I called the BBC and inquired about him. His name, they told me, was Peter Townsend, and they gave me his telephone number. It was that simple.

I arranged a meeting with Peter and we got along very well. He liked America and thought Americans were wonderful people. He had visited Florida several times and thought American business was the envy of the world. We were open with one another (well, as open as a businessman can be). It was like a first date: He knew that I was keen to buy, and I knew he was keen to sell. By the end of the first meeting, we were good friends.

Peter started as a computer programmer in the National Health Service (NHS). He had come across an unpublished study by the NHS that showed how the sale of newly-created private health insurance policies would impact hospital admissions and outpatient activities. Private insurance was becoming a popular perk for company executives: It was a handy way of jumping the inconvenient waiting lists for the free medicine of the NHS. Things occurred to Peter when he saw in the report that the government allowed surgeons to spend some allotted time doing private work in order to supplement their incomes. The government encouraged people to use private hospitals to relieve the pressure on government beds. In turn, companies were keen to offer private health insurance as a perk. There was only one thing missing: where were the doctors going to admit their patients? There were no private beds outside of London.

Peter was able to scrape enough money together to build a 25-bed surgical hospital in Surrey, just outside London. But he had to give up 33 percent of his business to a construction company that had agreed to build an additional five hospitals.

When we decided to purchase Peter's company, it had two operating hospitals and three under construction.

Peter started with a "nonnegotiable" price. He also said he would make all records available for review, but only after receiving a letter of understanding from HCA. A team of five or six head-office corporate officers came to London to conduct detailed negotiations. The team was headed by Charlie Martin, the company's Rottweiler and acquisitions negotiator. Watching him in action was worth two years at Harvard Business School. He was a big, solidly-built man of 40, and his technique was incredible.

At the first meeting, Charlie introduced the subject by saying, "Peter, you've got all the boys over here all excited about your company. They can't wait to get their hands on it. I personally don't like the deal, but they all do so I'm caught in the middle."

This got Peter worried that "the boys over here" weren't the real decision makers. Worried was how Charlie wanted him at the start of the negotiations. Then Charlie reassured him: "Peter, I'm here to do a deal, not to destroy a deal."

With Charlie and his four lieutenants from Nashville, a high-powered local legal firm, and an accounting firm on one side of the table, and Peter Townsend and his finance director on the other, poor Peter was outnumbered and outgunned. Charlie whittled away at the details of every aspect of the contract until poor Peter was slowly worn down. Every time he thought he could go out and celebrate his newfound wealth, Charlie started again — a few thousand here, a few thousand there. Charlie was buying and he was having fun. Peter was frustrated, impatient, and just wanted to go to dinner. I really thought he would simply walk away from the table.

Finally, only one item remained, worth £20,000. Charlie said, "Peter, it's late and we're all tired. I don't want to argue with you and I don't want to spoil the deal. Why don't we just flip a coin for this £20,000. After all, we are talking about a few million." Charlie won the toss, then quickly got up and shook Peter's hand. "Peter, I've just made you a multimillionaire."

"I've worked fucking hard for it," Peter said.

We went out to dinner. Everyone got along well and everyone was happy with the deal. Charlie made Peter pay for dinner.

And so our presence in England got off to a solid start. Once again, God had looked down on David Egee and smiled. My penance was Libya; my reward was England.

That's how Dale and I ended up in London, where we will remain until our ashes are taken back to Newtown to be buried alongside my mother, father, brother, and whoever else requires space in the meantime.

After two years of wanting to go to boarding school, Eliza finally got her wish. We sent her to Dover College, a high school on top of the famous white cliffs of Dover. Coming from Mediterranean cultures, she found the English students rather reserved. "They never touch one another when they talk," she said. Her best friend turned out to be a young girl from Brazil.

Dale once again went out house hunting. A real estate agent showed her an attractive two-story apartment in Cheyne Place, Chelsea, which adjoined the very fashionable Cheyne Walk along the Thames. The agent went on and on about how the property was owned by Sir John and Lady Aird. Every other word was "Lady this" and "Lady that." The name-dropping was supposed to add value to the property. We knew nothing about either English aristocracy or the meaning of titles. We only knew that they were people above our station in life and were somehow better than us. Dale was very nervous about meeting the owners: How does one address a Lady? Were they related to the Queen? Lady Aird turned out to be an attractive young mother of three children with a disarmingly direct manner. "Hello, I'm Margaret Aird. You must be Dale. You can call me Maggie." Dale was immediately put at ease.

The apartment was very English and looked directly into the famous Royal Physic Garden (the seeds to plant the cotton in Virginia came from these gardens). The apartment was freshly painted, had lots of light, and three good size bedrooms. Dale said, "I love it. We'll take it. But I want it all painted white." Lady Aird was a little surprised. "Oh, you don't like the green?" But she accepted our offer.

My first year working in England was very daunting. The 1,000-year old history, kings and queens, titled people with double-barreled names, civil servants appointed by the queen, dinner jackets, lounge suits, smoking jackets, black tie, and carriages at midnight — I was accustomed to working with people in pajamas and rags on their heads and civil servants with falcons perched on their arms. I came from an environment where I was known as an expert. My reputation as the director of the American University Hospital went before me. Now, I was placed in an environment that was even more foreign, and funny English was spoken.

I used to be a big fish in a small healthcare pond. Now I was thrown into a very big and unfamiliar pond and I didn't even know how to swim. We were faced with an audience that was known worldwide for its healthcare system. We were to meet people whose healthcare systems were emulated by other first-world countries. And we were there to show them that the private way was better (well, for those who could afford it, anyway).

It was only after three years in England that Dale and I began to feel at ease in the country. I started to ask myself why we would want to live elsewhere. We imagined remaining in England for the rest of our lives. In 1984, at the age of 48, I decided to become a British subject and applied for citizenship. I was feeling less and less like an American. I never missed anything American. We made fewer and fewer visits to America, for shorter and shorter periods of time. It was not a case of leaving America. It was more that I committed myself to a different part of the world that seemed more suited for me. In 1986, I swore allegiance to the Queen. A few years later, Dale did the same.

All our friends and acquaintances thought we were becoming British subjects because of some tax advantage. That wasn't the case. But travelling around Europe and even the Middle East was easier with a British passport. Contrary to popular perception, we were also able to retain our American citizenship. British citizens becoming Americans seemed to be culturally acceptable, but Americans becoming British subjects, while not unknown, was clearly novel.

HCA was a success in Britain. In 1987, after eight years, we owned and operated nine hospitals and five nursing homes. The hospitals were profitable and doing very well. We had recruited an excellent group of local managers who learned the American way of operating hospitals. We had no trouble attracting good medical doctors to our staff, all of whom seemed to enjoy our management style.

Nonetheless, HCA decided to accept an offer "they could not refuse" from a British health insurance company that was a nonprofit organization and the largest medical insurer at the time. It was an interesting alignment: The company insured the individual and then used its hospital facilities when people needed to use their insurance.

After the buyout, all of the Americans returned to the United States. We decided to stay. I didn't feel that returning to America was a realistic option. We had stayed overseas for too long. I resigned from HCA and converted my share options into cash, receiving $200,000.

Over the years, we became good friends with Sir John and Lady Aird. A short while after we moved in, they invited us to their "farm" in Gloucestershire. It was a far cry from any farm in Connecticut. They had about 500 acres of land and a large, lovely stone house. It was in the middle of the Cotswolds, thought by some to be the most beautiful part of England. We were to go for the weekend. Lady Aird said that they would be having a dinner party on Saturday evening.

At the same time, we became friendly with Charlie and Judy, the Duke and Duchess of Linlithgow. They lived just above us. When Dale told Judy that we were invited for the weekend, she told Dale to assume that the dinner would be formal — black tie and long dresses. I asked Charlie where I could rent a tux. "Buy one, my boy," he told me. "If you are going to be living in London and at this address, you'll need one often." Charlie's instructions were: "Arrive for tea between four and five, not later. Depart immediately after Sunday lunch."

At tea in the Aird's house, Margaret asked Dale if she could see her dress. Dale thought it would be fun to go a little ethnic but Margaret saw her choice and said, "Oh dear, you can't wear that. Come let me see what I have in my closet." After dinner, the women were supposed to excuse themselves to "powder their noses" while the men stayed behind, lighting their cigars and having a glass of port or brandy, served in glasses made for John's father by a Venetian glassmaker. In order to "appreciate the bouquet of the brandy," instead of being round, they were oval, Dale was in animated conversation with the two men on either side. She had to be asked twice to go get her nose powdered. In spite of this, we became lifelong friends, though Dale's relationship with John was more comfortable than with Margaret.

John was an engineer from Oxford University and a graduate of the Harvard Business School. Among other businesses, he owned and operated a successful manufacturing company. He was an entrepreneur and a financial genius.

I had been thinking about starting a small nursing home chain and wondered if John would be interested in forming a partnership with me. I showed him a copy of the accounts from one of our nursing homes. He said he would think about it.

When he came back to me, he had a business plan with a detailed budget projection based on three nursing homes over a five-year period. We each put in $200,000 as equal partners. Sitting around his dining room table one evening, John asked what we should call our company. Margaret, Dale, and I made suggestions. John was relatively quiet. Then he said, "What if we named it after Dale and called it DaleCare?"

We were an incredible double act. John provided the numbers and connected us to his finance contacts; I told the story of what we were doing and how. We told our story well and venture capitalists, investment banks, pensions funds, and commercial banks liked it. We were able to raise funds to purchase and refurbish three nursing homes with a total of 116 beds. One of them was a 19th century vicarage, another a 19th century mansion, and the third, a private residence from the same period. All three properties were completely renovated and substantial extensions were added.

Being in England provided Dale with a real opportunity to develop her Egee Art Consultancy. Her Dubai experience with the Hyatt Regency and the conference center was an excellent platform from which to take her business to greater heights. She would work from England, but restrict her market to the Middle East. It turned out that international companies actually preferred to work with English companies. Her Middle Eastern clients had more faith in the honesty, efficiency, and financial viability of Western European and American consultancy companies than ones that were locally situated.

Dale had to once again hit the ground running. She found premises appropriate for an art consultancy business just around the corner from where we were living. It was a 1,000 square foot artist's studio with excellent gallery space and enough room for an ever increasing, back office staff. Dale made contact with all the major architectural offices and large international hotel chains. The contacts she had from her tapestry business days were a big help.

She knew Hans Sternick and his family from the days when he was the vice-president responsible for all the Intercontinental Hotels in the Middle East. He went on to become president of the entire operation, working out of New York. The Sheraton hotel asked her to provide all the art for a new hotel and conference center in Doha, Qatar. She installed all the art in the Mobil Oil company offices in Riyadh, Saudi Arabia. While she was doing this, the vice president for Mobil Saudi Arabia invited the American ambassador to their office. He was so impressed that he arranged for Dale to meet with Vercan Wofter, who headed up the office responsible for furnishings for all US embassies and ambassadorial residences in Europe and the Middle East.

Based on her background and experience, Dale was chosen to provide the artwork for eight new US embassies, including Saudi Arabia, Egypt, Abu Dhabi, Kenya, Tanzania, Israel, Bangladesh, and Qatar. In carrying out her work, she visited almost every country in the Middle East and many parts of America and Western Europe. Dale's Egee Art Consultancy was becoming very successful, and at the time I was busy setting up DaleCare. Our priorities were in further developing our own careers so we agreed to live apart for a little while, putting our relationship into two days of the week.

In May 1986, John and I agreed that DaleCare would be set up and operated out of John's existing office building in Moreton-on-Marsh. He also arranged for me to rent a small cottage next door to their farm (estate was more like it) in Gloucestershire, so I could be close to work. I moved in there in September and stayed four nights a week.

It was an incredible estate, complete with stables. They had between five to eight horses and a groom to help look after them. One day, Margaret asked me if I had ever ridden a horse. "I tried once when I was little, but I was fearful and therefore not very good," I said. She asked if I would like to try again. My immediate response was yes. Margaret was an excellent rider, having started at age three. She was very professional and showed me exactly what to do. What surprised me most was that I was not afraid of the animal. I was cautious and a little anxious, but not afraid. Being just 50 years old, I was still fairly agile and quite coordinated. In fact, I had learned to ride a unicycle a few years earlier.

I enjoyed my first ride. It was exactly how I thought riding would be even when I was young. Margaret took me for a second ride and afterwards we agreed that I should take some serious riding lessons. I did and I loved it.

Learning to ride made my five days a week living alone much easier. My situation allowed me a wonderful opportunity to have my own horse and to have free use of the facilities of a properly run stable. I would wake to a glorious sunrise, then get on my horse and go over hedges and fences, across meadows and pasturelands, until I reached the top of the hill and looked down upon a distant stone village. To see a church spire poke through the low-lying mist on days like that was a beautiful experience and I felt privileged to have it.

On occasion, Margret would join me on my solo rides. I once confessed that I felt special when I was on a horse, that I felt better than the people below me. "That's why kings ride on horses," she said.

Margaret encouraged me to enter local horse events. I particularly liked jumping and cross-country events, so I was eager to try. Dressage was not my favorite. On such occasions, she helped get the horse and me looking appropriate. The horse had to be washed and brushed, its tail neatly plaited, hoofs painted, saddle and bridle polished.

"Where is your hat?" she'd scold me. "And don't forget to bring the sandwiches for our lunch. And what about your whip?" Margaret had gone through this routine before with her three children. She knew everybody at the event and knew every detail about the activity. She helped me avoid the "new boy" feeling that I had at each of my new prep schools. Margaret always introduced me to whomever she met, no matter how briefly, as "our friend, David Egee."

Thanks to John and Margaret, I always felt that my English experience was rather more special than that of most Americans working in England. I felt I was living out an English fantasy, which I quite enjoyed. I knew I was not accepted by the English upper class for the simple reason that I wasn't born into it. But I liked playing the part.

I was definitely part of John and Margaret's lives and to some extent, part of their routine. I knew where the drinks cabinet was and took the initiative to serve drinks if John was otherwise occupied. I was expected to clean up if the occasion called for it. I could be depended upon to sit next to or fit in between two difficult guests at the table. If it was the groom's day off, I knew how to bring in the horses from the paddock and where their feed was stored.

Margaret and I became good friends. We talked about everything. Wisely, she never spoke about my business dealings with John. But we were both doers: deadheading the roses on the southwest side of the house, walking the dogs over the hills, going to the market, picking up someone at the station, staying for supper (often with other guests). I was the extra man and played the role rather well, I think. If Margaret didn't agree, she never said anything to the contrary.

Dale was, and is, my wife and best friend. However, Margaret was a dear friend. She was a very pretty woman and she was good at the things she did, but her first priority was her family. She directed her children and did whatever she could to help them succeed at each stage of their lives. She developed a career for herself as a landscape designer and secured some excellent work, including a seven-year project for a wealthy couple in Nova Scotia, Canada. As a titled lady, she was conscious of her role in the community. She was a member of the parish council, she regularly did the flowers at the local church, and involved herself in the Girl Guides at the time her daughters were members. She worked in various community fundraising efforts and still had time for regular tennis matches with her husband, friends, and trainer.

My father visited once while I was living in the neighboring cottage. He too was struck by this "estimable" (his word) woman. He thought she was "pretty classy."

"I can see that you like her," he said. Then he added in a matter-of-fact way, "Are you having an affair with her?"

I said I wasn't. "I fantasize about it, but I know it would spoil a special relationship." Sometimes we would have dinner together without our spouses, perhaps like lovers might. There was a tension that existed between us, but I knew that it would not evolve any further.

DaleCare was profitable, but did not match our projections regarding return on capital. John Aird was not happy with the business. It was not the type of enterprise that suited his personality. He was an engineer and made his living owning and operating manufacturing companies. He saw businesses as an investment, and not a lifelong endeavor, and I was not able to properly manage the details of the business. As a result, John was forced to involve himself more in operational aspects than he had anticipated.

In 1989, Associated Nursing Services (ANS) made us a generous buyout offer. It would allow John and me to double our original investment. John took all of his money out of the business while I took enough out to make a down payment on our very first owned primary residence, with the balance held as 100,000 shares in ANS.

ANS was founded by Dr. Nick Dhandsa and his brother, Surinder, along with their friend, Anup, while Nick was still finishing his specialty training in pediatric medicine. In 1977, Nick became one of the youngest people to earn his MD license. When Nick wanted to purchase his first nursing home property, he asked his best friend, Anup, if his father would be willing to loan them £60,000. With these funds, Nick, Surinder, and the third co-founder, went to their local Barclays bank manager and asked if he would loan them £250,000. The manager reluctantly said that he would pass the request to the loan committee with a positive recommendation. He asked casually, "What does ANS stand for?"

"The A stands for Anup, N for Nick, and S for Surinder," said Nick.

"I can't take the application with ANS standing for you guys. Come up with a better name with the same letters."

The trio decided on the spot on Associated Nursing Services.

When Nick bought our three homes, he already had five, bringing his total to eight. Nick asked me what I planned to do now.

"I guess I'll start another company and do what I just finished doing again," I said vaguely.

Nick said that I was welcome to use his spare office in the meantime. He showed me a closet-sized cubicle with a small desk, chair, and phone. He introduced me to his secretary, Sandra, who said she could help if I needed anything. He didn't say another word, pretty much ignoring me as he appeared to ignore most people in the office.

A few weeks later, Nick called me to his office. "Why don't we have a little chat?" he suggested. He had raised some conditional funding to purchase six homes. Each had to be an existing, operational home, on a site large enough to build a substantial extension. The funding was available for only three months. One month had already passed. Surinder was the Marketing and Development Director. Nick wanted to split the responsibility. "I would like to offer you the job of development director," he said.

I was back in business. As fast as I could find a deal, Nick would find the money. I invested half of what I got from the sale of DaleCare and spent the next seven years working at ANS. I was doing what I did best: finding projects and seeing them through. It is a very satisfying feeling to do what you enjoy and to get paid for doing it. It was a wonderful way to end my career.

Two very important things shaped my career with ANS. The first was Margaret Thatcher's vision of England. It was the age of privatization: the railways, coal mines, steel mills, airlines, and other industries were sold off. If she couldn't sell something, such as the National Health Service or prisons, she at least allowed the private sector to provide services on a contractual basis to various government departments. The best and biggest example of this was in the National Health Services (NHS). The NHS was sacred to the voters and she knew it. But she wanted to make it more efficient. Thatcher did not see the NHS as a free cradle-to-the-grave service, and she set about closing long-stay psychiatric and geriatric hospitals. She also closed geriatric wards in all small "cottage hospitals." These residents were pushed back to their families or to local social services. With our nursing home experience and financial resources, we were able to provide the required nursing home care. And we had a ready-made demand.

The second event was a meltdown of the housing market and the commercial property business. ANS was able to buy sites or unfinished developments at favorable prices. We easily got planning permissions for new developments because we created employment. For each bed, we needed to employ one individual. A 100-bed nursing home required 100 employees.

As a result, business was booming. By the time I retired in 2006, at the age of 70, sold my shares in the company, and Dale closed her business, we were able to establish a fund that allowed us to spend our retirement pretty much as we wished.

Looking back, I realize I was best suited as an employee and not an entrepreneur. In Beirut, I may have thought that I wanted to be out in the rough-and-tumble Middle East, but in the end, a traditional, well-mannered and more predictable (if less profitable) way of doing business suited me best. I had to admit that I'd sooner have the umbrella of a large business structure than work for myself.

Towards the End

> "To be able to fill leisure intelligently is the last product of civilization and at present very few people have reached this level."
>
> ~ Bertrand Russell

Cancer starts as something minor. Taking a pee one morning, I noted some blood in my urine. My GP thought it was a urinary tract infection and treated it with antibiotics. The blood stopped and I was feeling no pain. But when it returned a month later, he sent me to Dr. Woodhouse, a urologist. I assumed that in the worst case scenario, it would be a kidney infection.

Cancer

The urologist asked me to describe my symptoms along with a history of previous illnesses and the health of my parents. In looking back, I unknowingly neglected to tell him that my grandfather had had bladder cancer. He took some blood for various tests and we arranged a follow-up appointment. I thought everything would be fine.

When I returned to his office five days later, I was his last appointment of the day. I was keen to make it as short as possible in order to join Dale at a cocktail reception that evening. As you can imagine, I was totally unprepared for what he told me.

"I have reviewed the results of your blood tests and you have cancer."

It was as simple as that. I had no obvious reaction except that my hands were suddenly sweaty. "Are you sure these are my test results?" I asked.

"Yes, I am sorry to say they are." He quickly moved the conversation on to what to do next. He didn't allow me to dwell on the word "cancer." It is a powerful word, a dreadful word.

We talked about the various treatments: radiation therapy, chemotherapy, or surgery. I picked up on the drift of his conversation and surgery seemed the best option. He said the sooner we did it the better it would be, as the cancer had already penetrated the second lining of my bladder. Since it was a matter of some urgency, surgery was scheduled for two weeks later.

I liked Dr. Woodhouse's manner. He was straightforward, but understanding. He had a no-nonsense persona about him, but was at the same time genuinely concerned. I felt comfortable putting my life in his hands. I didn't feel the need for a second or third opinion; I just wanted to get on with it. That evening, I contacted my brother-in-law, a hematologist. "The prognosis for the cancer of the bladder is good — better than a lot of others," he told me. Despite the awful nature of the diagnosis, I had a feeling that I would get better. I couldn't believe that I was going to die just yet.

If you remove a man's bladder, you need a new way for the urine to be stored and discharged. There are two options. However, in my case, the doctor said that I was a good candidate for a "Mainz II modified ureterosigmoidostomy."

"We will create a new bladder from your lower bowel," he explained. "I will then redirect the ureters to lead from your kidneys into the newly created bladder. So, instead of urinating from your penis, you will have to urinate out of your backside."

"You mean I will never be able to fart again?"

"Only when you're on the toilet."

I was concerned. "How many of these things have you ever done?" I asked.

"Oh, about fifty-three. They are not suitable for all patients, but it'll allow you a better lifestyle than an external bag." That was little comfort. I didn't particularly fancy a "lifestyle" that required that I spend the rest of my life urinating like a girl. No more running behind a tree or standing with my back to the road. But I preferred that to an external plastic bag tethered to a tube running down the side of the stomach.

I went into the hospital on September 20, 2002, and remained there until early February 2003. At one point, my doctor said, "In your case, anything that could go wrong did." I got the chills, fever, and infections. The ureter wouldn't bind into the new bladder and, just for good measure, my stomach collapsed. Those are just some of the complications I remember. But over that period, we established a good rapport. It has been ten years since I had the procedure, but I still have an annual check-up; just to make sure that things are alright and no new cancer has developed.

Soon after my discharge, I started worrying. "Dr. Woodhouse," I said. "I can't seem to get an erection anymore." It was a big concern.

"I removed your bladder, your prostate, and your urethra, but I did not remove your libido," he said. And I remembered a long time ago my father deemphasized the importance of a penis in having a good sex life. I left the doctor's clinic feeling only slightly reassured. When I got home, I suggested to Dale that we go to our house in France later that year. When we got there, I spent most of my time lying in the wonderful, warm sunshine. I could feel that I was actually beginning to get better.

One afternoon, I was lying on a chaise lounge on the terrace, just off the kitchen. The sun was high in the sky. It was hot, but with a cool breeze. My mind was at ease. As was my habit, I was sunbathing in my underwear, adjusting my private parts, as men tend to do. Feeling quite relaxed, I started to massage myself. It felt very good. I did not want to stop. I had my first orgasm in six months. It went from the bottom of my heels to the top of my head.

I thought it strange that Dr. Woodhouse never mentioned that particular sequence of events. Until this time, the entire area was numb. There was no life — I had lost interest. By removing my urethra, in my own mind I was castrated. Now, in spite of destruction and restructuring, I was never able to get an erection again. But I can still have an orgasm.

Dale and I were able to pick up our sex life from where we had left off some eight months earlier. It was the start of a wonderful new adventure with 20-minute orgasms.

Dementia

Misplacing your keys is normal behavior as you grow older. Putting them in the refrigerator is dementia.

The term dementia describes a condition where a variety of different brain functions — memory, recognition, language, planning, and personality — start to deteriorate over time. It is not part of the normal aging process, but it is a common disease. Some 700,000 people in the UK alone have it. Alzheimer's disease is one form of dementia. In 2013, an estimated 5.2 million Americans of all ages had Alzheimer's disease.

Dale and I spend six months of the year in Olmet. It was while we were there in 2005, when Dale was 71, that she became aware of the deterioration of her memory and that she was feeling less able to deal with stressful situations. She always said, "I have never been famous for my memory," which she accepted as part of her makeup.

That summer, we were putting on a special reception for the mayor and people of the village and surrounding areas. We were expecting about 60 guests. The occasion was a celebration of the restoration of the village chapel tower. That morning, Dale took me aside. "David, I just can't seem to cope," she told me. "I don't want to be involved in any preparations. I can't deal with it." Looking back, that was the point where I felt something was wrong. Mrs. Egee not participating in a social event? She had a reputation among all her friends, relatives, and colleagues as an enthusiastic, gracious, and generous hostess. I brushed this aside and made appropriate excuses for Dale.

Later, she played it down. "I guess I can't do what I used to do. But don't forget, I'm over 70 and getting older," she said. To me, she had not changed. She was still beautiful and lively, just like she was in Beirut, Dubai, Rome, Libya and England. She had recently returned from a two-week tour of Palestine, visiting camps, slums, and refugee centers, just as she had always done.

Previously, I had missed the signs of an unhappy first wife and now I was missing the signs of an ageing second wife. I should have realized that something was wrong much earlier.

As time went on, Dale got increasingly concerned about her forgetfulness and was becoming aware that she was withdrawing slightly from her busy social life. In 2009, our GP referred Dale to the geriatric psychiatry department of the Chelsea Westminster Hospital. She had a three-hour mental cognitive test and a brain scan. When Dale returned to the hospital three weeks later, the doctor casually asked her, "Well, how did you enjoy your morning of tests?"

"What tests?" she asked.

"You had a battery of tests and a brain scan." Dale did not remember. The doctor told her that the verbal tests and the brain scan confirmed that she was "in the early stages of Alzheimer's." He prescribed a medication called "Aricept." It would not reverse or stop the disease, but it would slow its progression. We both knew her character would change. It might take a long time, but it would happen. I would need to adapt to these changes.

"Alzheimer's" is as powerful a word as "cancer." I don't know which one is more frightening. And even though we were expecting the former, it's still unnerving when the verdict is announced. I must confess that I was rather blasé about the confirmed diagnosis. Perhaps I was in denial: Dale couldn't have Alzheimer's! She had a little memory loss, maybe she was a little confused sometimes, but *not* Alzheimer's. So what if she couldn't take on as many duties as before?

We were sanguine about the announcement. I don't mean we were optimistic about Dale getting better. We understood there was no cure. But we agreed that a sense of humor would be the best way to deal with the condition. We also did not want to be in denial about her condition and decided not to try to hide it in any way. Should our family and friends become aware of changes in Dale's behavior, it would be easier to discuss it openly than to pretend everything was normal, especially when it wasn't. Dale felt that if people were aware of her situation, they would be more understanding. In my mind, I kept rehearsing words like patience, tolerance, understanding, and love.

Of the 50 nursing homes we owned and operated, about 20 had centers for elderly, mentally-infirm patients in various stages of Alzheimer's. The units were specifically designed to accommodate people who were easily confused and tended to wander. For example, the design of the main corridor was such that it "never ended." Alzheimer's patients tend to get anxious, angry, and frustrated if they "can't get out." So the main corridor was circular, with nursing services in the middle. Their doors were colored and illustrated, rather than numbered. Patients wore identity bracelets with a set of alarms where necessary, and they were encouraged to enter the matron's offices. Oftentimes, they would sit in on meetings, coming and going as they wished. Now, when I look back at these units, I can see Dale's future and my own. To be frank, it is, at best, a problematic one.

I started to realize that Dale was becoming more vulnerable to the outside environment. Her computer security was compromised on three occasions in six months. She fell for telephone marketing ploys. She was more easily misled and confused as to a stranger's intentions. She needed reassurance of my devotion to her. She accepted her mental state, but needed to be told that she was coping and could manage.

Some of Dale's new behavioral characteristics have become a permanent part of her personality. Over the past few years, I noticed that she enjoys talking with strangers. She will find ways to start a dialogue. She will tell a man digging the road what a hard job he has, having to work in such weather, or ask a beggar how he is managing and suggest what he could do to earn money. She will tell the bus driver what a wonderful job he's doing and get into a long discussion with a taxi driver that will last the entire way to our destination. She sees it as "spreading joy" to those she can engage. How can I fault that?

Perhaps most obvious is the forgetting. As people grow older, they have "senior moments," usually involving relatively unimportant pieces of information. It's customary to forget proper names and words. But in Dale's condition, names and places are not only forgotten, they become confused. She confuses her brother with her first husband. She permanently forgets the name of someone she knew well and saw often. It is as if she never knew the person. If I remind her of the details, she still may not know about whom I'm talking. Other times, we agree that I will make a BLT for dinner. But when I come home from the office, she has purchased a ready-roasted chicken. Or if I ask her whether she remembered to pick up the shallots I requested, she'll say, "They're in the fridge."

"You mean these?" I ask, holding up the fresh produce.

"Yes."

"But Dale, these are leeks."

"Well, what are shallots?"

It is remarkable because Dale was a superb cook and used to read cookbooks like novels.

On another occasion, Dale lost her membership cards to nearly every major museum in London. They're plastic, like credit cards. She immediately went to the bank and cancelled her debit and credit cards as well as mine, even though they were in her purse. Nevertheless, we still have a good laugh together over some of her moments of confusion.

A recent amusing incident: Dale had a rash accompanied by a terrible itching. It had been going on for two months while doctors tried to find the cause. On one particular occasion, we decided to Google "itching." Included in the information was that calamine lotion inhibits itching. At one time, I used it when I got poison ivy while living in Connecticut (funny, it doesn't seem to grow in Europe). We agreed, together, that Dale go to the chemist the following morning to get the calamine lotion. When I arrived back home, Dale announced that she'd gotten the "camomile tea" I'd asked her to buy. We enjoyed that little gaffe.

For now, Dale's condition is quite innocuous. She is often as amused by it as I am. The more harmful characteristics are yet to come: acts of aggression, getting seriously lost, or being a danger to herself or others, the latter of which is too distant to cause me concern at this time. But recently, she got angry:

Last summer, Dale went to our bank to draw some funds out of our account. She came home very upset because our account had been "wiped out."

"What do you mean, 'wiped out'?" I asked.

"Someone has hacked into our account."

I asked what she meant. But the more questions I asked, the more anxious she became. "Why are you challenging me?" she countered angrily.

We went to investigate together, and it turned out that she had gone to an entirely different bank.

According to a British Medical Association publication, "Patients will experience changes in behavior, including eating and sexual patterns." But it goes on to say, "It has to be remembered at all times that the behavior is due to the disease and not the patient." The last time Dale and I made love was on December 9, 2009, three weeks after Aricept was prescribed. I remember the day, the month, and the time. The change in our habits was so upsetting to me that I asked a pharmacist friend if he could check whether this was a side effect of Aricept. The response to his inquiry from the makers of the drug was, "There have been such reports, but the number was of no statistical significance."

This has been the most troubling revelation for me. The sexual aspect of our relationship was a marvel of joyful intimacy. This situation has in no way affected our love and devotion for one another. I'm only happy that she wasn't diagnosed before 2009.

Dale feels most comfortable when talking about the past. She spends hours going through old files of her companies' activities, reviewing her old appointment diaries, and looking at our old photos. She spends a lot of time rereading her 307-page typewritten, single-spaced "Beirut Journal," which covers the seven years of our life in Lebanon.

Dale is beginning to withdraw more from the lifestyle she previously thrived on. Her social life is becoming more confined. I can feel the dynamics of our relationship altering. She has started to depend more on me than ever before. Our social life was always dictated by Dale; now it is organized by me. I am also more involved in everyday domestic affairs.

I encourage Dale to do things on her own. I want to discourage her from depending on me too much. Reliance is addicting — the difference is to know when one needs the drug and when one would simply like to have the drug.

Most of the time when Dale's computer does not work, it can be fixed by turning the machine off and on again. I insist on explaining to her how simple it is. Our French GP says she may never learn. But she can do so many other things, he says. He gets the same complaints from other caregivers. He tells them: "His/her brain works differently now. It may not be the way you want it to work."

Another dependency issue is on the horizon: driving. Dale's favorite toy in the world is her little Smart car. It gives her independence in our rural French environment. My children chastise me for allowing her to drive. "Do you think it's a good idea that she still drives?" Eliza asks.

Perhaps she shouldn't be driving. And perhaps she is a danger to herself and others. But I also feel that most males under the age of 40 are just as dangerous behind the wheel.

"I'm going to let her drive as long as she likes."

"What if she has an accident?"

"Driving thirty miles per hour, it won't be serious," I respond.

Now our daughter thinks both her parents have Alzheimer's.

There is only one way to deal with a partner who has a degenerative disease and that is to think of the good things. When I worry, I give myself a pep talk: "David, when you think about your future with Dale, you worry. You should not. Be happy for her. She's not frightened by isolation. In fact, she now wants to minimize her social life. She has no worries for the future. She has someone she loves — adores, in fact. She has a family and two wonderful places to live. She believes she is very rich. Most importantly, she has a super strong faith in God. Be happy for her and be thankful that you have an understanding of the disease. And please, stop reading about Alzheimer's."

Retirement

In earlier times, people didn't expect to live very long after they retired. Social Security payments in the United States started in 1935. The retirement age was 65; and this was arbitrarily decided for pragmatic reasons based on the current Private Pensions Schemes and the Federal Railroad Retirement System. At that time, the average life expectancy was 61 years. However, as the average lifespan approaches 78 today, the retirement age remains at 65. The concept of retirement has created different expectations. At this time, it's a so-called "third age," a 17-year bonus on the average life. So how do we fill this 17-year gap "intelligently," as Bertrand Russell once asked?

Fortunately, rather than sit on a park bench feeding the pigeons, watch daytime television, or passively react to daily necessities and trivia, I am just intelligent enough to make a rational plan. At all costs, I wanted to avoid sitting in waiting rooms with a blank stare, like a dog waiting in the shade for nothing in particular. I am going to be proactive. I spent my first five winters writing this book, and I have spent the last five summers repairing, renovating, and remodeling our house in France. My book is finished and our house in France is nearly done.

I realize that retirement is not an extended holiday that goes on for years. I want it to be another period in my life. I have successfully gone through childhood (with a few problems) and adolescence (which I seemed to have enjoyed more than most of my friends). I passed through young adulthood — and am now starting older adulthood. Lastly is death, and it is my intention to plan this intelligently rather than passively without control.

I have a friend who announced to me that in his retirement he feels he has done nothing and he fully intends to do nothing of any consequences. He says:

"I am happy doing nothing and I am not a burden on society, so why do I have to do something just to keep occupied? I wake up in the morning and read about what other people are doing. I do this over a leisurely breakfast — I sit and enjoy the relatively mild activities going on in and next to the Thames. I wake without an alarm clock." He told me: "My life doesn't necessarily require a structure, I don't need any goals, and I'm not concerned about facing new challenges. I don't feel my life is tedious. If something comes along, I may show some interest, but if nothing comes along, that interests me, too. I have no dreams and no goals."

As a rule, people don't change very much after puberty. What they were like at that time is replicated in retirement. Those who reach retirement and then look back on their lives and careers and think: "Wasn't I lucky? Wasn't life good?" These people have a better chance of seeing their retirement in a positive light. In any case, most people don't think about retirement beforehand.

My career defined who I was and where I placed myself in a social order within a community. I wanted status and recognition and my work provided me with it. I worked with, and had contact with, everyone from Syrian day laborers living in culverts to managers and directors of large and small businesses, presidents of universities and corporations, and heads of various ministerial departments.

I woke up every morning and loved what I was doing. As Steve Jobs said shortly before he died: "If you're going to be successful, you have to love your work." I remember driving my car from a meeting with a health authority official to the job site of a nursing home under construction, saying to myself: *This isn't really work. I'm not working, I'm having too much fun.* Before I was 65, I often wondered how I would possibly live without working. I worked just about my whole life starting as a boy delivering milk, not because my family needed the money, but because I wanted more money than my childhood allowance accorded. I think about that period in my life when my "job" was going to school every day. I wasn't successful every day, but for some reason I kept at it. I can't say that I loved my job at the time. But I knew it was a way to a career that I would like when I "grew up." I knew instinctively, not unlike the gazelle and the lion, I had to "wake up running." And if I did, there would be a reward at the end. I think my attitude toward work was rather unsophisticated. I never thought very much about it and never asked, "Why am I doing this?" or "Is this really what I want to do?" Work came to me naturally.

I wanted to work until I was 70. When I was about 35, I bought a small pension policy that was structured to start on the day I retired at the age of 70. At age 67, having been diagnosed with cancer, it looked like I wasn't going to retire at age 70, a milestone I set for myself. Told by my surgeon that the procedure for removing my bladder and the convalescent period would last at least six months, I didn't believe him. Surely not that long. But, of course, the surgeon was right.

I worked on a consultancy basis. I was responsible for getting a cosmetic surgical clinic operational and obtaining the necessary registration requirements. I went back to work, pleased with my new challenge. After obtaining the required certifications for the clinic, I started our annual four-week holiday at our house in France. I always looked forward to this break in our routine. I loved our summers in the South of France; it was the only time that most of our family could come together in one place at one time. This was the first year of my working life I felt I needed a holiday. It wasn't a case of wanting a change; I wanted to start doing something other than work. It was the first holiday break when I was not "on call." I didn't want to go back to work; I still wanted to wake up early, but I didn't want to "run" as much. The idea of retiring is not as fretful as I believed it might be, but I had to find something to fill the void. That's when I got the idea about writing my memoirs.

Dying/Death

As I write this, in two months' time I will reach the average life expectancy of a male living in England today, so I am about to start living on "borrowed time."

When I first retired and started to write my life story, I had, as Maurice Zundel wrote: "The fear of the abyss which grips a person who, at the end of his life realizes that he missed out on what really mattered." Having now finished my story and gone back through my life, I don't feel I have missed out at all. I am at ease with the thought of death. My only concern is the contemporary process by which we die — the "just before dying" progression of events. It's the months that I might lose control of my life by being immobilized: waiting for others to feed me, take me to the toilet, and having someone to wipe my bottom. Or, my walking naked along a corridor carrying my own shit to the nursing station. Circumstances I have witnessed. Staff encouraging patients to eat by touching a nerve at the back of the throat so the reflex will allow the food to flow. Lying in bed, mouth half open and eyes closed, with visitors and nurses not knowing if I am dead or alive — with no one able to help me finish the process of dying.

Just before reaching her 80th birthday, Dale was diagnosed with aortic valve stenosis. After three days of tests, the cardiac surgeon and two of his young assistants came to the foot of her bed to say that they had completed her tests and confirmed the diagnosis. A short discussion followed. As she had already been diagnosed with early symptoms of Alzheimer's, Dale wondered if cardiac surgery was not contraindicated?

"Yes, it is," said the surgeon. "But we've tested you, and your score was an acceptable 6/10; we don't operate on anyone who is over 8." Dale hesitated; she appeared to be drifting off. Later, she told me that she'd thought about our friend Nelson, who'd had an open-heart operation at exactly her same age, 80. After three attempts, he found a doctor willing to perform an open-heart operation. After the procedure, he was discharged to a nursing home where he spent the rest of his life, incapable of caring for himself.

"On the other hand," said the doctor, "you may be a candidate for a trans-catheterization and avoid open heart surgery." Dale had no immediate response, just as the doctors would expect from someone faced with this medical dilemma. Finally, she spoke. "Do you believe in God?" The surgeon said nothing. Dale pointed her finger at the junior of his two assistants and said in an accusing fashion, "Do you believe in God?" The young surgeon looked to the senior consultant for help. Dale replied for him, "I believe in God. And my faith is strong and when I die I know I'm going to Heaven. Hence, I am not afraid of dying and, therefore, I am not having any surgery."

Three days later I received a letter from the surgeon's secretary asking if I would please reply in writing that my wife did not want to continue treatment. Two weeks later we returned to France and had a meeting with a senior cardiologist, who is also a good friend. He agreed with her decision completely and added that he had a number of patients who were in the same situation and that she could live a long time. Gradually, as time went by, she would find activities to be more difficult and she would feel more tired.

I believe there are two reasons a person takes his own life. The first is to run away from it — to escape loneliness, to avoid a depressed state that cannot be reversed. In such cases, the taking of one's life is a tragedy.

A second reason for taking one's life is more positive. It is almost the opposite of the above. Taking one's own life is part of a life plan. It is controlling one's own destiny. It is a question of carrying out one's own wishes. And in my father's case, it was a choice. It was, in fact, an expression of carrying out his last choice. He was not depressed. He was not sad and lonely. He was simply weary of living.

I did not personally witness the following; however, my sister, Elaine, told me about it in some detail:

About 18 months before my father died, he began to arrange his affairs. His life was always orderly and he wanted this to continue after his death. He wanted to avoid complications and confrontations between family members. He wanted no unanswered questions or obstacles remaining after his death.

He sold his house and invited an antique dealer to sell any furniture of particular value. He set certain items aside, those in which one of us had expressed particular interest. He selected a date and we joined him at the house. We picked numbers from a hat. Whoever got number one could pick one item he wanted. Then number two picked an item and so on, until all the items had been selected. Anything left over was given to charity. All his assets were converted to shares on the stock market with instructions to sell on the date of his death and divide the proceeds equally among his children. He rented a small apartment in an elderly care complex. When he died, his only remaining possession was an old Volkswagen car.

As my father went from growing old to being old, he realized he had less and less to contribute. He had spent his life treating bodies, prolonging lives, and giving advice to improve lives. He knew his body was running down.

Visits to the doctor and urgent visits to the emergency room became more frequent. He was no longer entering the hospital through the door marked "Medical Staff," but through the main entrance of the emergency room. He had been chief of the medical staff for ten years but now, he was just another aged patient clogging up the medical care system.

He had several problems that were typical of a body that had functioned for over 90 years and was gradually deteriorating, not acute, but debilitating. He was coughing up blood from small ulcers. These in turn caused anemia. He also had multiple pulmonary emboli, which cannot be reversed. Medication would not improve the quality of his life. He was alive, but not living. It was a question of simply prolonging survival — but for what? To move from a walker to a wheelchair, and finally, to being bedridden. Throughout his professional life, he had witnessed difficult deaths and he was unwilling to face this himself under any circumstances and, hence, anticipated his own death.

He had seen many people die from accidents, shootings, wounds, and natural causes. He understood that the rest of his life would be spent between ignorance and distraction. It would be one accident after another, one error after another. It was a life of being left for hours in his own urine. It meant being surrounded by people with empty eyes, all waiting for death to occur. He knew what the future held.

At the age of 90, he felt the time had arrived for him to do what he had always planned to do. Since we were very young, he'd spoken about his "two pills" and his intention of taking his own life. The pills he took were Tuinal — a combination of seconal and phenobarbital, and just in case of stomach upset, Tums tablets.

It was about 6:00 PM, the traditional hour our entire family gathered for dinner before our father started his evening office hours. He telephoned the oldest and the youngest of his five children, who lived only a short distance away. My sister said he spoke in a calm, matter-of-fact way. "I've decided to take my two pills tonight. Could you come over this evening and ask Paul to come with you?" They arrived at around 7:00. He was lying on the bed when they entered his room. They talked about inconsequential things of the day.

He got up, went to the bathroom, changed into his pajamas, and took his two pills. When he returned to bed, Elaine was sitting on the side of the bed next to his pillow. She put her arm around his head. Paul sat on a chair at the end of the bed.

When he took the tablets, he immediately started to cough. He said, "Wouldn't it be funny if I choked to death instead?" A sense of irony to the end.

He instructed them to leave his small apartment after he fell asleep and to leave the door unlocked.

Elaine's husband, Peter, became a doctor at my father's encouragement. He went to the same medical school, and they worked together at the same hospital. He was not only a son-in-law, but also a close professional colleague. My father phoned Peter and said, "If something should go wrong, I'd like you to come over." Peter agreed to do so.

"Thanks, Pete, and thanks for the past thirty-five years that we've worked together."

My father settled his head in Elaine's arms. She could tell that he was beginning to feel sleepy. He told her that he had never imagined such a wonderful life, a life he was able to make for himself. She said he seemed pleased with his success and the opportunities he was given. As a child, his mother insisted that he learn to play the violin. Strangely, he had mentioned specifically how pleased he was to hear the violinist, Jascha Heifetz, play in Carnegie Hall and to see Arturo Toscanini conduct. He never mentioned his children or his wife.

And then he just seemed to drift off to sleep. Elaine said he appeared pleased and happy that he was leaving. They did exactly what he had instructed them to do, leaving the apartment when he became unconscious and deliberately leaving the door unlocked.

The following morning around 10:00, the phone rang. It was Mr. Honnan of Honnan's Funeral Home. He said to Elaine, "I had a meeting arranged with your father. There was no answer, but I saw his car in the drive. I tried the door and went in… I'm very sorry to tell you… Would you like me to make the necessary arrangements?"

I was not unhappy when he died. I couldn't feel any sorrow. In fact, I was pleased for him that it went so well. I didn't have a single sorrowful moment. He died knowing there was nothing more he wanted to do, whereas my mother had a sudden and severe stroke while dressing for the theatre. She had much more growing old to do. She was taken away from us. It was not her choice. Not so in our father's case.

My father was the most important individual in my life. He influenced my development in almost every way. His belief in me and his dedication to my education got me through the most difficult 14 years of my life. In many ways, I have wanted to imitate him.

The way he conducted the end of his life is exactly the way I intend to orchestrate my own demise.

Epilogue

I've come to the end of my story.

Each one of us identifies with a generation that is particular to our lives. For me, I was fortunate enough to have lived in the mid '50s and right through the '60s. World War II had ended five years earlier and America was starting over. It was the beginning of "Car Culture" and rebellion. Getting my driving license in 1952 allowed me to participate. It was a time of relaxation. Certain social taboos such as living openly together, using birth control measures like "the pill," and the interdicting of recreational drugs such as marijuana had started to crumble. The young woman, aged 22, who has been doing my typing, thinks my generation was "Sooo cool."

It's funny; some moments in life seem significant at the time, but when reviewed, don't stand out as much. For example, while writing this book, I forgot about the time someone tried to rob me at the Hilton Hotel in New York. I ran after him, stark naked, and tackled him in the middle of the hotel corridor, something I was afraid to do at Rumsey Hall School. When I complained to the head of night security, it turned out the man who tried to rob me was the head of night security! I also forgot about the Harley Davidson I owned in my retirement, but had to give up after falling off it twice. Making patchwork materials, getting a pilot's license, being a jockey, riding a unicycle, and publishing photography are other pastimes I haven't included in this book — amusing and significant at the time, but in hindsight, lesser accomplishments.

After four long winters, working every year from October to April, it is time to stop. I could continue this project for another four winters, and by then I'd be 81. That's three years past my statistical lifetime.

The project has become a task. I started it as a way of filling my time while I got accustomed to retirement. Writing my memoirs seemed like the ideal challenge. After all, if the *New York Review of Books* advertises 275 new publications in a single monthly issue and if libraries are stuffed with books, writing couldn't be that difficult.

But it ended up being a burden, a commitment to people I know and to myself. I feel a little like the mouse that said, "I'm no longer interested in the cheese. I just want out of the trap."

But now that I've decided to stop, I'm right back where I started, needing "something to do." I'm not sure what it might be, but you can bet it will be anything but writing another book. I'll do something that comes more naturally, something that makes me continue to feel unique or unusual. The first idea that comes to mind is reawakening my interest in photography. I want to be an amateur photojournalist and portrait photographer during the summer months; and, in the winter months, process and print the images. Taking random photos is commonplace; the advent of digital has made everyone a "half-decent" photographer; not an original one, mind you, just a half-decent one. Websites with excellent images and nothing to differentiate them abound. An artist/architect friend of mine suggested I develop themed photo assignments, like Matthew Brady's Civil War photos or William Claxton's jazz photography. Successful composers find great melodies; good photographers focus on a given subject and perfect it over a period of time. So, I take back my previous statement — perhaps I will publish a book of images instead of words.

I'm basically a conformist who wants to be a nonconformist. If I could stand outside of myself, I'd declare: "That's the way I want to spend the rest of my life." I could go on and on about how things "used to be." There were always better educational systems — manners were better, crime was less, children behaved better — and, of course, wives were always better in the old days.

Right now, I feel good about myself and, therefore, I make people around me feel good. Over and over in our nursing homes, I witnessed the reaction of patients or residents to people with a positive personality. In our homes, the staff always engaged in a more positive manner with the patients who had a positive outlook. They would avoid, as much as possible, those with a grumpy and negative outlook.

As my friends die off or become "grumpy old men," I want to be different. I want to stay in touch with the next generation, continually challenging myself in constructive ways.

Printed in Poland
by Amazon Fulfillment
Poland Sp. z o.o., Wrocław